JUNIOR GREAT BOOKS

SERIES 3

BOOK TWO

◆   ◆   ◆

The interpretive discussion program that moves

students toward excellence in reading comprehension,

critical thinking, and writing

JUNIOR GREAT BOOKS®

SERIES 3   BOOK TWO

THE GREAT BOOKS FOUNDATION

A nonprofit educational organization

Copyright © 2006 by The Great Books Foundation

Chicago, Illinois

All rights reserved

ISBN 978-1-933147-03-1

9   8   7

Printed in the United States of America

Published and distributed by

THE GREAT BOOKS FOUNDATION

A nonprofit educational organization

35 East Wacker Drive, Suite 400

Chicago, IL 60601

CONTENTS

"I'm going to learn how to weave dreams."

THE DREAM WEAVER

Concha Castroviejo

Rogelia was a good-for-nothing little girl. That was what her sisters and her schoolmistress said.

She was asked questions at school about the day's lesson, and she was so busy daydreaming she didn't know what she was being asked; at home they told her to iron handkerchiefs so that she'd learn how to do the ironing, and she burned them; to fill the coffee cups at meals, and she spilled coffee on the tablecloth; to water the plants, and the water dripped all over the floor.

"This girl is very clumsy," said her sister Camila, who was very capable and quite conceited.

"This girl is stupid," her sister Pepa would add.

"There's no telling whether this girl will learn or not," the schoolmistress sighed.

The worst of it was that Rogelia never learned how to make bobbin lace. Her granny, her sisters, and her aunts—all the women in her house—were very skillful with the bobbins and made beautiful lace with stars, birds, and flowers, fashioning all sorts of whimsical designs with the threads. This pleased Rogelia a great deal. She would sit down beside her granny, with her little sewing cushion full of pins, threads, and bobbins on her knees, and begin to dream of making wonderful designs. But she dreamed of her designs so intently, and planned them in her head so enthusiastically, that the bobbins collided, tangling the threads; the pins fell out of place, undoing the knots; and her handiwork ended up a sorry mess.

Rogelia burst into tears and felt ashamed as her older sisters began reprimanding her.

"Go get the tissue paper ready to wrap up our lacework," Camila would say to her. "That's all you're good for."

And that was how things went for Rogelia every day.

One afternoon she was peering out the window and saw a very old woman pass by the house, gazing at the sky. Rogelia, who was a very well-mannered girl, ran to the door and

went out into the street, because it seemed that the old woman was about to trip and fall. But the old woman laughed and said to her, "Don't worry. I'm looking at the clouds. By doing so, the work I do later on turns out so nicely."

"What sort of work do you do?" Rogelia asked her.

The woman answered, "I'm a weaver of dreams."

Those words excited Rogelia.

"What a fine occupation!" she exclaimed, and then she asked, "What is your name, señora?"

"My name is Gosvinda."

Rogelia would have liked to follow along after old Gosvinda, but she did not dare. She remained at the door watching her, and saw her walk all the way down the long street, leave the town, and go into the woods. From that day on, Rogelia thought only of the dream weaver. At school she was more and more inattentive; she burned more and more clothes as she did the ironing, spilled more and more water as she watered the flower pots, and made an even worse tangle of the pins, threads, and bobbins when she sat down alongside her granny to make lace.

"This girl is going to have to be sent to a boarding school to see if they can manage to teach her something," her sister Pepa said one day.

"A place where they keep her locked up and punish her," her sister Camila added.

"Where they won't allow her to while away her time gazing at clouds," Pepa piped up again.

"She isn't good for anything," her aunt said.

Then Rogelia said to her sisters, "Since I must learn something, I'm going to learn how to weave dreams."

And her sisters laughed at her.

But Rogelia packed two changes of clothes, a jacket, and her rain boots into a cardboard box, put on a bonnet that she kept to wear on feast days, gave her granny a goodbye kiss, and took off on her own.

Rogelia left the town and reached the woods. It was dark there because the tops of the trees were so dense. Rogelia walked on for a long time until at last she came upon an open meadow, and in the meadow was a house with its walls painted pink and its windows green, surrounded on every side with yellow flowers. The house had seven chimneys through which poured out lovely smoke that looked like no other, a different color puffing out from each chimney.

Rogelia pushed on the door, which was unlocked, and went into the house. From the kitchen, she climbed up to a bedroom, and from the bedroom, she climbed up to the loft, and from the loft, she saw the clouds and mountains in the distance. Old Gosvinda worked there in the loft all day, weaving one dream after another. The smoke of the dreams was what was escaping by way of the chimneys.

On reaching the loft, Rogelia said, "Good day, Señora Gosvinda."

The weaver was not surprised to see the little girl.

"I knew you'd come," she said, answering her greeting.

Rogelia looked all around. She saw the distaffs
and the looms with threads of crystal, gold, and
silver, with threads the color of emeralds and
sapphires. In one corner there were twelve mice
grooming their whiskers.

"I've come to stay, if you'll allow me to," she
said to Gosvinda. "I wish to learn to weave
dreams. At home they tell me I'm useless, but it
may be that I'm suited for such a wonderful
occupation."

Gosvinda replied that she could stay and
explained to her that she needed a girl to help
her because she had a great many orders to fill.
People kept needing more and more dreams.

Rogelia remained in the house in the woods.
Very early each morning, she went up to the loft

and learned to thread the looms and ready the tufts to be spun into threads on the distaff. The threads glided in and out until they formed the weft under the old weaver's hand, and the distaff spun faster and faster, raising a breeze that made the mice sneeze. During the day the cuckoos, and at nightfall the swifts, came and went through the window, bringing in their beaks the orders sent by princes from their royal palaces and by miners from the depths of their caves. All the men and women who knew the weaver ordered dreams from her.

"Once upon a time there used to be seven of us weavers," Gosvinda said to Rogelia, "but my companions retired to take their rest and left me by myself. They were older than I. When I grow weary and retire, there will be no one left at all."

"And what will people do then?" Rogelia asked.

"They'll manufacture pills so they can have synthetic dreams. And children will weave their own dreams for themselves."

Little by little, Rogelia learned to make lovely woven fabrics of the color and shape of clouds. She learned how to make the rainbow tarry by

singing to it, and how to wrap it up in orange-colored dreams. She learned to weave pink and blue dreams for the young, and green ones to console those who were sick and those who were sad. And white dreams so that children could embroider them in color.

"You're a very clever little girl," old Gosvinda told her.

And that made Rogelia feel very happy.

"Oh, my!" she replied. "If only those back home could see me!"

"They would still find you useless. If you say you weave dreams, people will laugh at you."

•••

Dreams, once they were woven, came out of the chimneys in a lacework of smoke, and the wind blew them to distant houses. Rogelia soon learned to sweep the floor and to put pots on the fire. Every week a bear brought old Gosvinda wood, rabbits took care of supplying her with vegetables, and blackbirds arrived with fruit.

"What a beautiful house!" Rogelia sighed.

Rogelia learned the weaver's craft so well that dreams now held no secrets for her. Because she worked with them so much with her hands, they no longer lodged in her head. She paid careful attention to the thin, fragile threads, to the delicate interweaving formed by the branches of the trees and the patterns made by the clouds, and to the colors of the rainbow that appeared above the sharp-pointed roof of the little house. Rogelia's mind was never in a daze now, for the dreams were no longer in her head, but in her hands. "When I want a dream for myself," she thought, "I shall weave the most beautiful one that has ever existed."

One day old Gosvinda said to her, "In order to find out if this is your true calling, you must put it to the test: return home and work there."

Rogelia realized that she was obliged to
obey. She went to her cardboard box and put
on a dress that she had woven with the leftovers
from the distaff tufts and that gleamed with the
colors of flowers.

Rogelia returned home, greeted everyone, and
said that she had been learning to be capable. In
the beginning her sisters laughed at her, but
Rogelia's hands were blessed. If she sat down to
make bobbin lace, the bobbins crossed back and
forth like castanets and the threads turned into
lace, with birds, flowers, and clouds in the white
background that looked like a snow-covered

field. If she watered the plants, she did not spill a single drop. If she ironed, the glistening garment looked as good as new.

Everyone sang Rogelia's praises. The meters of lace she made were sought after by all the townspeople. For the grand fiesta of the year they ordered decorations for the balconies from her.

But Rogelia could no longer live without dreams. Each day she climbed to the very top of the house to see if she could make out the smoke coming from the chimneys of Gosvinda the weaver's house.

Rogelia readied her cardboard box once again, bade everyone goodbye, and headed for the woods one morning as day broke.

•••

"Good day!" she said as she entered the loft.

The weaver was seated in her corner, and the mice were holding in place the tufts that she was putting on the distaffs.

"I knew you would come," she said, answering Rogelia's greeting. "Now you will stay here forevermore."

Rogelia remained with old Gosvinda. She welcomed the cuckoos and the swifts, fed the mice, helped the bear unload the wood, and placed the vegetables and fruit that the rabbits and the blackbirds brought into their proper baskets. But above all, she kept weaving and weaving. She wove the most complicated and difficult dreams, the ones that tired old Gosvinda. She attended to everything, for she had so many dreams in her hands that none were left in her head. She was so fond of her dreams and so proud of her work that she never dared to keep them.

Each year she went to the town to visit her grandmother, her sisters, and her aunt. She greeted them and then went off once again.

One day a very serious looking gentleman, carrying a large briefcase full of registers with black oilcloth covers, came knocking at the door of Gosvinda's house. Rogelia came down from the loft to see what he wanted, and the gentleman told her that he had come to find out who lived there and what their occupation was, so he could write their names down in the tax registers.

"Old Gosvinda and I live here," Rogelia explained to him, "and we are weavers of dreams."

The gentleman looked through his registers and said that such an occupation was not on any list. Then he cleared his throat and left.

Jean Labadie was the most popular storyteller.

Jean Labadie's Big Black Dog

*French-Canadian folktale
as told by Natalie Savage Carlson*

Once in another time, Jean Labadie was the most popular storyteller in the parish. He acted out every story so that it would seem more real.

When he told about the great falls in Niagara, he made a booming noise deep in his throat and whirled his fists around each other. Then each listener could plainly hear the falls and see the white water churning and splashing as if it were about to pour down on his own head. But Jean Labadie had to stop telling his stories about the *loup-garou*, the demon who takes the shape of a terrible animal and pounces upon those foolish people who go out alone at night.

Every time the storyteller dropped
down on all fours, rolled his eyes,
snorted, and clawed at the floor,
his listeners ran away from him
in terror.

It was only on the long winter
evenings that Jean had time to tell
these tales. All the rest of the year,
he worked hard with his cows and his
pigs and his chickens.

One day Jean Labadie noticed that his flock
of chickens was getting smaller and smaller.
He began to suspect that his neighbor, André
Drouillard, was stealing them. Yet he never
could catch André in the act.

For three nights running, Jean took his gun
down from the wall and slept in the henhouse
with his chickens. But the only thing that
happened was that his hens were disturbed by
having their feeder roost with them, and they
stopped laying well. So Jean sighed and put his
gun back and climbed into his own bed again.

One afternoon when Jean went to help his
neighbor mow the weeds around his barn, he
found a bunch of gray chicken feathers near

the fence. Now he was sure that André was taking his chickens, for all of his neighbor's chickens were scrawny white things.

He did not know how to broach the matter to André without making an enemy of him. And when one lives in the country and needs help with many tasks, it is a great mistake to make an enemy of a close neighbor. Jean studied the matter as his scythe went swish, swish through the tall weeds. At last he thought of a way out.

"Have you seen my big black dog, André?" he asked his neighbor.

"What big black dog?" asked André. "I didn't know you had a dog."

"I just got him from the Indians," said Jean. "Someone has been stealing my chickens so I got myself a dog to protect them. He is a very fierce dog, bigger than a wolf and twice as wild."

Jean took one hand off the scythe and pointed to the ridge behind the barn.

"There he goes now," he cried, "with his big red tongue hanging out of his mouth. See him!"

André looked but could see nothing.

"Surely you must see him. He runs along so fast. He lifts one paw this way and another paw that way."

As Jean said this, he dropped the scythe and lifted first one hand in its black glove and then the other.

André looked at the black gloves going up and down like the paws of a big black dog. Then he looked toward the ridge. He grew excited.

"Yes, yes," he cried, "I do see him now. He is running along the fence. He lifts one paw this way and another paw that way, just like you say."

Jean was pleased that he was such a good actor he could make André see a dog that didn't exist at all.

"Now that you have seen him," he said, "you will know him if you should meet. Give him a wide path and don't do anything that will make him suspicious. He is a very fierce watchdog."

André promised to stay a safe distance from the big black dog.

Jean Labadie was proud of himself over the success of his trick. No more chickens disappeared. It seemed that his problem was solved.

Then one day André greeted him with, "I saw your big black dog in the road today. He was running along lifting one paw this way and another paw that way. I got out of his way, you can bet my life!"

Jean Labadie was pleased and annoyed at the same time. Pleased that André believed so completely in the big black dog that he could actually see him. He was also annoyed because the big black dog had been running down the road when he should have been on the farm.

Another day André leaned over the fence.

"Good day, Jean Labadie," he said. "I saw your big black dog on the other side of the village. He was jumping over fences and bushes. Isn't it a bad thing for him to wander so far away? Someone might take him for the *loup-garou*."

Jean Labadie was disgusted with his neighbor's good imagination.

"André," he asked, "how can my dog be on the other side of the village when he is right here at home? See him walking through the yard, lifting one paw this way and another paw that way?"

André looked in Jean's yard with surprise.

"And so he is," he agreed. "My faith, what a one he is! He must run like lightning to get home so fast. Perhaps you should chain him up. Someone will surely mistake such a fast dog for the *loup-garou*."

···

Jean shrugged hopelessly.

"All right," he said, "perhaps you are right.
I will chain him near the henhouse."

"They will be very happy to hear that in the
village," said André. "Everyone is afraid of him.
I have told them all about him, how big
and fierce he is, how his long red
tongue hangs out of his mouth, and
how he lifts one paw this way
and another paw that way."

Jean was angry.

"I would thank you to leave
my dog alone, André Drouillard,"
he said stiffly.

"Oh, ho, and that I do,"
retorted André.
"But today on the
road he growled
and snapped at me.
I would not be
here to tell
the story if I
hadn't taken
to a tall
maple tree."

Jean Labadie pressed his lips together.

"Then I will chain him up this very moment." He gave a long low whistle. "Come, fellow! Here, fellow!"

André took to his heels.

Of course, this should have ended the matter, and Jean Labadie thought that it had. But one day when he went to the village to buy some nails for his roof, he ran into Madame Villeneuve in a great how-does-it-make of excitement.

"Jean Labadie," she cried to him, "you should be ashamed of yourself, letting that fierce dog run loose in the village."

"But my dog is chained up in the yard at home," said Jean.

"So André Drouillard told me," said Madame, "but he has broken loose. He is running along lifting one paw this way and another paw that way, with the broken chain dragging in the dust. He growled at me and bared his fangs. It's a lucky thing his chain caught on a bush or I would not be talking to you now."

Jean sighed.

"Perhaps I should get rid of my big black dog," he said. "Tomorrow I will take him back to the Indians."

So next day Jean hitched his horse to the cart and waited until he saw André Drouillard at work in his garden. Then he whistled loudly toward the yard, made a great show of helping his dog climb up between the wheels and drove past André's house with one arm curved out in a bow, as if it were around the dog's neck.

"*Au revoir*, André!" he called. Then he looked at the empty half of the seat. "Bark goodbye to André Drouillard, fellow, for you are leaving here forever."

Jean drove out to the Indian village and spent the day with his friends, eating and talking. It seemed a bad waste of time when there was so much to be done on the farm, but on the other hand,

it was worth idling all day in order to end the big black dog matter.

Dusk was falling as he rounded the curve near his home. He saw the shadowy figure of André Drouillard waiting for him near his gate. A feeling of foreboding came over Jean.

"What is it?" he asked his neighbor. "Do you have some bad news for me?"

"It's about your big black dog," said André. "He has come back home. Indeed he beat you by an hour. It was that long ago I saw him running down the road to your house with his big red tongue hanging out of his mouth and lifting one paw this way and another paw that way."

Jean was filled with rage. For a twist of tobacco, he would have struck André with his horsewhip.

"André Drouillard," he shouted, "you are a liar! I just left the big black dog with the Indians. They have tied him up."

André sneered.

"A liar am I? We shall see who is the liar. Wait until the others see your big black dog running around again."

•••

So Jean might as well have accused André
of being a chicken thief in the first place,
for now they were enemies anyway. And he
certainly might as well have stayed home
and fixed his roof.

Things turned out as his neighbor had hinted.
Madame Villeneuve saw the big black dog
running behind her house. Henri Dupuis saw
him running around the corner of the store.
Delphine Langlois even saw him running
through the graveyard among the tombstones.
And always as he ran along, he lifted one
paw this way and another paw that way.

There came that day when Jean Labadie left
his neighbor chopping wood all by himself,
because they were no longer friends, and drove
into the village to have his black mare shod.
While he was sitting in front of the
blacksmith shop, André Drouillard
came galloping up at a great speed.
He could scarcely hold the reins,
for one hand was cut and
bleeding.

A crowd quickly gathered.
"What is wrong, André
Drouillard?" they asked.
"Have you cut yourself?"
"Where is Dr. Brisson?
Someone fetch Dr. Brisson."
André Drouillard pointed
his bleeding hand at Jean
Labadie.
"His big black dog bit me,"
he accused. "Without warning,
he jumped the fence as soon as Jean drove
away and sank his teeth into my hand."
There was a gasp of horror from every throat.
Jean Labadie reddened. He walked over to
André and stared at the wound.

"It looks like an ax cut to me," he said.

Then everyone grew angry at Jean Labadie and his big black dog. They threatened to drive them both out of the parish.

"My friends," said Jean wearily, "I think it is time for this matter to be ended. The truth of it is that I have no big black dog. I never had a big black dog. It was all a joke."

"Aha!" cried André. "Now he is trying to crawl out of the blame. He says he has no big black dog. Yet I have seen it with my own eyes, running around and lifting one paw this way and another paw that way."

"I have seen it, too," cried Madame Villeneuve. "It ran up and growled at me."

"And I."

"And I."

Jean Labadie bowed his head.

"All right, my friends," he said. "There is nothing more I can do about it. I guess that big black dog will eat me out of house and home for the rest of my life."

"You mean you won't make things right about this hand?" demanded André Drouillard.

"What do you want me to do?" asked Jean.

"I will be laid up for a week at least," said André Drouillard, "and right at harvest time. Then, too, there may be a scar. But for two of your plumpest pullets, I am willing to overlook the matter and be friends again."

"That is fair," cried Henri Dupuis.

"It is just," cried the blacksmith.

"A generous proposal," agreed everyone.

"And now we will return to my farm," said Jean Labadie, "and I will give André two of my pullets. But all of you must come. I want witnesses."

A crowd trooped down the road to watch the transaction.

After Jean had given his neighbor two of his best pullets, he commanded the crowd, "Wait!"

He went into the house. When he returned, he was carrying his gun.

"I want witnesses," explained Jean, "because I am going to shoot my big black dog. I want everyone to see this happen."

The crowd murmured and surged. Jean gave a long low whistle toward the henhouse.

"Here comes my big black dog," he pointed.

"You can see how he runs to me with his big red tongue hanging out and lifting one paw this way and another paw that way."

Everyone saw the big black dog.

Jean Labadie lifted his gun to his shoulder, pointed it at nothing and pulled the trigger. There was a deafening roar and the gun kicked Jean to the ground. He arose and brushed off his blouse. Madame Villeneuve screamed and Delphine Langlois fainted.

"There," said Jean, brushing away a tear, "it is done. That is the end of my big black dog. Isn't that true?"

And everyone agreed that the dog was gone for good.

CAPORUSHES

English folktale
as told by Flora Annie Steel

Once upon a
time, a long, long while ago,
when all the world was young
and all sorts of strange things
happened, there lived a very rich gentleman
whose wife had died, leaving him three
lovely daughters. They were as the apple of
his eye, and he loved them exceedingly.

Now one day he wanted to find out if they
loved him in return, so he said to the eldest,
"How much do you love me, my dear?"

And she answered as pat as may be, "As I
love my life."

"Very good, my dear," said he, and gave her a kiss. Then he said to the second girl, "How much do you love me, my dear?"

And she answered as swift as thought, "Better than all the world beside."

"Good!" he replied, and patted her on the cheek. Then he turned to the youngest, who was also the prettiest.

"And how much do *you* love me, my dearest?"

Now the youngest daughter was not only pretty, she was clever. So she thought a moment, then she said slowly, "I love you as fresh meat loves salt!"

Now when her father heard this he was very angry, because he really loved her more than the others.

"What!" he said. "If that is all you give me in return for all I've given you, out of my house you go." So there and then he turned her out of the home where she had been born and bred, and shut the door in her face.

Not knowing where to go, she wandered on, and she wandered on, till she came to a big fen where the reeds grew ever so tall and the rushes swayed in the wind like a field of corn. There she sat down and plaited herself an overall of rushes and a cap to match, so as to hide her fine clothes and her beautiful golden hair that was all set with milk-white pearls. For she was a wise girl and thought that in such lonely country, mayhap, some robber might fall in with her and kill her to get her fine clothes and jewels.

It took a long time to plait the dress and cap, and while she plaited she sang a little song:

Hide my hair, O cap o' rushes,
Hide my heart, O robe o' rushes.
Sure! my answer had no fault
I love him more than he loves salt.

And the fen birds sat and listened and sang back to her:

Cap o' rushes, shed no tear,
Robe o' rushes, have no fear.
With these words if fault he'd find,
Sure your father must be blind.

When her task was finished she put on her robe of rushes, and it hid all her fine clothes. And she put on the cap, and it hid all her beautiful hair, so that she looked quite a common country girl. But the fen birds flew away, singing as they flew:

Cap o' rushes! we can see,
Robe o' rushes! what you be,
Fair and clean, and fine and tidy,
So you'll be whate'er betide ye.

By this time she was very, very hungry, so she wandered on, and she wandered on. But ne'er a cottage or a hamlet did she see, till just at sunsetting she came on a great house on the

edge of the fen. It had a fine front door to it, but mindful of her dress of rushes she went round to the back. And there she saw a strapping fat scullion washing pots and pans with a very sulky face. So, being a clever girl, she guessed what the maid was wanting and said, "If I may have a night's lodging, I will scrub the pots and pans for you."

"Why! Here's luck," replied the scullery maid, ever so pleased. "I was just wanting badly to go walking with my sweetheart. So if you will do my work you shall share my bed and have a bite of my supper. Only mind you scrub the pots clean, or Cook will be at me."

Now next morning the pots were scraped so clean that they looked like new, and the saucepans were polished like silver, and the cook said to the scullion, "Who cleaned these pots? Not you, I'll swear." So the maid had to up and out with the truth. Then the cook would have turned away the old maid and put on the new, but the latter would not hear of it.

"The maid was kind to me and gave me a night's lodging," she said. "So now I will stay without wages and do the dirty work for her."

So Caporushes—for so they called her since she would give no other name—stayed on and cleaned the pots and scraped the saucepans.

Now it so happened that her master's son came of age, and to celebrate the occasion a ball

•••

was given to the neighbourhood, for the young
man was a grand dancer and loved nothing so
well as a country measure. It was a very fine
party, and after supper was served, the servants
were allowed to go and watch the quality
from the gallery of the ballroom.

But Caporushes refused to go, for she also was
a grand dancer, and she was afraid that when
she heard the fiddles starting a merry jig, she
might start dancing. So she excused herself by
saying she was too tired with scraping pots
and washing saucepans, and when the others
went off she crept up to her bed.

But alas! And alack-a-day! The door had been
left open, and as she lay in her bed she could
hear the fiddlers fiddling
away and the tramp
of dancing feet.

Then she
upped and off
with her cap
and robe of
rushes, and there
she was, ever
so fine and tidy.

She was in the ballroom in a trice, joining in
the jig, and none was more beautiful or better
dressed than she. While as for her dancing . . . !

Her master's son singled her out at once and
with the finest of bows engaged her as his
partner for the rest of the night. So she danced
away to her heart's content, while the whole
room was agog, trying to find out who the
beautiful young stranger could be. But she kept
her own counsel and, making some excuse,
slipped away before the ball finished. So when
her fellow servants came to bed, there she was in
hers, in her cap and robe of rushes, pretending
to be fast asleep.

Next morning, however,
the maids could talk of
nothing but the beautiful
stranger.

•••

"You should have seen her," they said. "She was the loveliest young lady as ever you see, not a bit like the likes o' we. Her golden hair was all silvered with pearls, and her dress—law! You wouldn't believe how she was dressed. Young master never took his eyes off her."

And Caporushes only smiled and said, with a twinkle in her eye, "I should like to see her, but I don't think I ever shall."

"Oh, yes, you will," they replied, "for young master has ordered another ball tonight in hopes she will come to dance again."

But that evening Caporushes refused once more to go to the gallery, saying she was too tired with cleaning pots and scraping saucepans. And once more when she heard the fiddlers fiddling she said to herself, "I must have one dance—just one with the young master: he dances so beautifully." For she felt certain he would dance with her.

And sure enough, when she had upped and offed with her cap and robe of rushes, there he was at the door waiting for her to come. For he had determined to dance with no one else.

•••

So he took her by the hand, and they
danced down the ballroom. It was a sight of all
sights! Never were such dancers! So young,
so handsome, so fine, so gay!

But once again Caporushes kept her own
counsel and just slipped away on some excuse in
time, so that when her fellow servants came to
their beds they found her in hers, pretending
to be fast asleep; but her cheeks were all flushed
and her breath came fast. So they said, "She is
dreaming. We hope her dreams are happy."

But next morning they were full of what she
had missed. Never was such a beautiful young
gentleman as young master! Never was such
a beautiful young lady! Never was such beautiful
dancing! Everyone else had stopped theirs to
look on.

And Caporushes, with a twinkle in her eyes,
said, "I should like to see her, but I'm *sure* I
never shall!"

"Oh yes!" they replied. "If you come tonight
you're sure to see her, for young master has
ordered another ball in hopes the beautiful
stranger will come again. For it's easy to see
he is madly in love with her."

•••

Then Caporushes told herself she would not dance again, since it was not fit for a gay young master to be in love with his scullery maid. But, alas! The moment she heard the fiddlers fiddling, she just upped and offed with her rushes, and there she was, fine and tidy as ever! She didn't even have to brush her beautiful golden hair!

And once again she was in the ballroom in a trice, dancing away with young master, who never took his eyes off her and implored her to tell him who she was. But she kept her own counsel and only told him that she never, never, never would come to dance anymore, and that he must say goodbye. And he held her hand so fast that she had a job to get away. And lo and behold! His ring came off his finger, and as she ran up to her bed there it was in her hand! She had just time to put on her cap and robe of rushes, when her fellow servants came trooping in and found her awake.

"It was the noise you made coming upstairs," she made excuse. But they said, "Not we! It is the whole place that is in an uproar searching for the beautiful stranger. Young master he tried to detain her, but she slipped from him like an eel. But he declares he will find her, for if he doesn't he will die of love for her."

Then Caporushes laughed. "Young men don't die of love," said she. "He will find someone else."

But he didn't. He spent his whole time looking for his beautiful dancer, but go where he might, and ask whom he would, he never heard anything about her. And day by day he grew thinner and thinner, and paler and paler, until at last he took to his bed.

And the housekeeper came to the cook and said, "Cook the nicest dinner you can cook, for young master eats nothing."

Then the cook prepared soups and jellies and creams and roast chicken and bread sauce, but the young man would none of them.

And Caporushes cleaned the pots and scraped the saucepans and said nothing.

Then the housekeeper came crying and said to the cook, "Prepare some gruel for young master. Mayhap he'd take that. If not he will die for love of the beautiful dancer. If she could see him now, she would have pity on him."

So the cook began to make the gruel, and Caporushes left scraping saucepans and watched her.

"Let me stir it," she said, "while you fetch a cup from the pantry room."

So Caporushes stirred the gruel, and what did she do but slip young master's ring into it before the cook came back!

Then the butler took the cup upstairs on a silver salver. But when the young master saw it he waved it away, till the butler, with tears, begged him just to taste it.

So the young master took a silver spoon and stirred the gruel, and he felt something hard at the bottom of the cup. And when he fished it

up, lo, it was his own ring! Then he sat up in
bed and said quite loud, "Send for the cook!"

And when she came he asked her who made
the gruel.

"I did," she said, for she was half-pleased and
half-frightened.

Then he looked at her all over and said,
"No, you didn't! You're too stout! Tell me who
made it and you shan't be harmed!"

Then the cook began to cry. "If you please,
sir, I *did* make it. But Caporushes stirred it."

"And who is Caporushes?" asked the young
man.

"If you please, sir, Caporushes is the scullion," whimpered the cook.

Then the young man sighed and fell back on his pillow. "Send Caporushes here," he said in a faint voice, for he really was very near dying.

And when Caporushes came he just looked at her cap and her robe of rushes and turned his face to the wall. But he asked her in a weak little voice, "From whom did you get that ring?"

Now when Caporushes saw the poor young man so weak and worn with love for her, her heart melted, and she replied softly, "From him that gave it me," and offed with her cap and robe of rushes. And there she was as fine and tidy as ever, with her beautiful golden hair all silvered over with pearls.

And the young man caught sight of her with the tail of his eye, and sat up in bed as strong as may be, and drew her to him and gave her a great big kiss. So, of course, they were to be married in spite of her being only a scullery maid, for she told no one who she was.

Now everyone far and near was asked to the wedding. Among the invited guests was Caporushes' father, who from grief at losing his favourite daughter had lost his sight and was very dull and miserable. However, as a friend of the family, he had to come to the young master's wedding.

Now the marriage feast was to be the finest ever seen. But Caporushes went to her friend the cook and said, "Dress every dish without one mite of salt."

"That'll be rare and nasty," replied the cook. But because she prided herself on having let Caporushes stir the gruel and so saved the young master's life, she did as she was asked and dressed every dish for the wedding breakfast without one mite of salt.

Now when the company sat down to table their faces were full of smiles and content, for all the dishes looked so nice and tasty. But no sooner had the guests begun to eat than their faces fell, for nothing can be tasty without salt.

Then Caporushes' blind father, whom his daughter had seated next to her, burst out crying.

"What is the matter?" she asked.

Then the old man sobbed, "I had a daughter whom I loved dearly, dearly. And I asked her how much she loved me, and she replied,

'As fresh meat loves salt.' And I was angry with
her and turned her out of house and home,
for I thought she didn't love me at all. But now
I see she loved me best of all."

And as he said the words his eyes were
opened, and there beside him was his daughter,
lovelier than ever.

And she gave him one hand, and her husband
the young master the other, and laughed, saying,
"I love you both as fresh meat loves salt." And
after that they were all happy forevermore.

"Time to start school," Mama tells me.

THE UPSIDE-DOWN BOY

Juan Felipe Herrera

1. Mama, who loves words, sings out the name on the
   street sign—Juniper. "Who-nee-purr! Who-nee-purr!"

2. Papi parks our old army truck on Juniper Street
   in front of Mrs. Andasola's tiny pink house.
   "We found it at last," Papi shouts, "Who-nee-purr!"

3. "Time to start school," Mama tells me with music in
   her voice.
   "My Who-nee-purr Street!" I yell to the chickens in
   the yard.

"Don't worry, *chico*,"
Papi says as he walks me to school.
"Everything changes. A new place has new leaves
on the trees and blows fresh air into your body."

I pinch my ear. Am I really here?
Maybe the street lamp is really a golden cornstalk
with a dusty gray coat.

People speed by alone in their fancy melting cars.
In the valleys, *campesinos* sang "*Buenos días*,
   Juanito."

I make a clown face, half funny,
half scared. "I don't speak English," I say to Papi.
"Will my tongue turn into a rock?"

I slow step into school.
My *burrito de papas*, my potato burrito, in a
   brown bag.
Empty playground,
fences locked. One cloud up high.

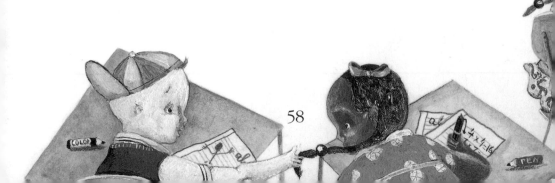

...

9
No one
in the halls. Open a door with a blue number 27.
"*¿Dónde estoy?*" Where am I?
My question in Spanish fades
as the thick door slams behind me.

10
Mrs. Sampson, the teacher, shows me my desk.
Kids laugh when I poke my nose into
    my lunch bag.

11
The hard round clock above my head
clicks and aims its strange
    arrows at me.

On the chalkboard, I see a row
of alphabet letters and addition numbers. If I
    learn them,
will they grow like seeds?

If I learn the English words,
will my voice reach the ceiling, weave through it
like grapevines?

We are finger-painting.
I make wild suns with my open hands.
Crazy tomato cars and cucumber sombreros—
I write my name with seven chiles.

"What is that?" Mrs. Sampson asks.
My tongue is a rock.

 The school bell rings
and shakes me.

I run and grab my lunch bag
and sit on the green steel bench.
In a few fast minutes, I finish my potato burrito.
But everyone plays,
and I am alone.

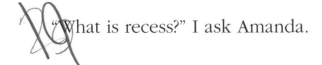

"It is only recess,"
my classmate Amanda says in Spanish.
In Spanish, I pronounce "recess" slowly.
"Sounds like *reses*—like the word for cattle,
huh?" I say.

"What is recess?" I ask Amanda.

...

The high bell
roars again.

This time everyone eats their sandwiches,
while I play in the breezy baseball diamond
by myself.

"Is this recess?" I ask again.

When I jump up,
everyone sits.
When I sit,
all the kids swing through the air.
My feet float through the clouds,
when all I want is to touch the earth.
I am the upside-down boy.

Papi comes home to Mrs. Andasola's pink house.
I show him my finger painting.
"What a spicy sun," he sings out.
"It reminds me of hot summer days in the
    San Joaquin Valley,"
he says, brushing his dark hair with his hands.

"Look, Mama!
 See my painting?"

"Those are flying tomatoes
 ready for salsa," Mama sings.
 She shows my painting to Mrs. Andasola,
 who shows it to Gabino, her canary.

"Gabino, Gabino, see?" Mrs. Andasola yells.
"What do you think?"
 Gabino nods his head back and forth.
 "*Pío, pío, piiiii!*"

28

Mrs. Sampson invites me
to the front of the class.
   "Sing, Juanito,
sing a song we have been
   practicing."

29

I pop up shaking. I am
   alone facing the class.

30

"Ready to sing?" Mrs. Sampson
   asks me.
I am frozen, then a deep
   breath fills me,
"Three blind mice, three
   blind mice," I sing.

31

My eyes open as big as the ceiling, and
   my hands spread out as if catching
   raindrops from the sky.

32

"You have a very beautiful voice, Juanito,"
   Mrs. Sampson says.
"What is beautiful?" I ask Amanda after school.

At home, I help Mama and Mrs. Andasola
make *buñuelos*—fried sweet cinnamon tortilla chips.

"Piiiiicho, come heeeere," I sing out,
calling my dog as I stretch a dough ball.

"Listen to meeeee," I sing to Picho with his ears
curled up into fuzzy triangles. "My voice is
beauuuuutiful!"

"What is he singing?" Mrs. Andasola asks my mom,
as she gently lays a *buñuelo* into the frying pan.

"My teacher says my voice is beauuuuutiful," I sing,
dancing with a tiny dough ball stuck on my nose.

"*Sí, sí,*" Mama laughs.
"Let's see if your *buñuelos* come out beautiful, too."

65

...

"I only made it to the third grade, Juanito,"
Mama tells me as I get ready for bed.

"When we lived in El Paso, Texas,
    my mother needed help at home. We were
        very poor
    and she was tired from cleaning people's houses."

"That year your mama won a spelling medal,"
Papi says as he shaves in the bathroom.

"Your Papi learned English without a school,"
    Mama says.
"When he worked the railroads, he would pay
    his buddies a penny for each word they taught him."

Papi says softly, "Each word,
each language has its own magic."

66

•••

After a week of reading a new poem aloud to
   us every day,
Mrs. Sampson says, "Write a poem,"
as she plays symphony music on the old red
   phonograph.

I think of Mama, squeeze my pencil,
pour letters from the shiny tip like a skinny river.

The waves tumble onto the page
Ls curl at the bottom.
Fs tip their hats from their heads.
Ms are sea waves. They crash over my table.

JUANITO'S POEM

Papi Felipe with a mustache of words.
Mama Lucha with strawberries in her hair.
I see magic salsa in my house
and everywhere!

68

...

"I got an A on my poem!" I yell to everyone
in the front yard where Mama gives Papi a
	haircut.

I show Gabino my paper
as I fly through the kitchen to the backyard.

"Listen," I sing to the baby chicks,
with my hands up as if I am a famous music
	conductor.

I sprinkle corn kernels and sing out my poem.
Each fuzzy chick gets a name:
"Beethoven! You are the one with the bushy
	head!
Mozart! You jumpy black-spotted hen!
Johann Sebastian! Tiny red rooster, dance,
	dance!"

69

In the morning, as we walk to school,
Papi turns and says, "You do have a nice voice,
    Juanito.
I never heard you sing until yesterday
when you fed the chickens.
At first, when we moved here,
you looked sad, and I didn't know what to do."

"I felt funny, upside down," I say to him.
"The city streets aren't soft with flowers.
Buildings don't have faces. You know, Papi,
in the *campo* I knew all the names, even of
    those bugs
with little wild eyes and shiny noses!"

"Here," he says. "Here's my harmonica.
It has many voices, many beautiful songs
just like you. Sing them!"

...

On Open House Day,
Mama and Papi sit in the front row.
Mrs. Andasola admires our drawings on the walls,
Gabino on her shoulder.

"Our paintings look like the flowery fields back
in the Valley," I tell Amanda.

"I have a surprise," I whisper to Mama.
"I am *El Maestro* Juanito, the choir conductor!"
Mrs. Sampson smiles wearing a chile sombrero
and puts on the music.

I blow a C with my harmonica—"La la la laaaaah!
Ready to sing out your poems?" I ask my choir.
"*Uno . . . dos . . .* and three!"

THE GREEN MAN

Gail E. Haley

*The story you are about to read may have happened
just this way—or perhaps it came about in a
different manner in some other place entirely. . . .*

Claude was the only
son of Squire Archibald.
He was arrogant, vain,
and selfish. He spent
most of his time hunting,
hawking, and riding about the
countryside in his fine clothes.

One evening Claude rode into
the village, and after ordering a lavish
meal at the Mermaid and Bush, he sat watching
the bustle of village life.

"Look at those ignorant peasants putting food out for the Green Man when they can barely feed their own children."

"They are grateful, Master Claude," replied the landlord. "For the Green Man keeps their animals healthy. He protects their children if they stray into the forest. Without him, the crops would not grow, nor the seasons turn in their course."

"Rubbish! Those are just silly tales. There is no Green Man!"

"Mind your tongue, sir," chided the landlord. "Terrible things can happen to those who make fun of old beliefs."

Some days afterward, Claude set out for a day's hunting. He never hunted on foot; he preferred to shoot from horseback. His men and dogs had gone ahead as beaters to drive the game toward him, but nothing was happening, and Claude grew tired of waiting. He rode deeper into the forest.

"Those beaters are incompetent. I haven't seen an animal all day!" he grumbled.

Soon Claude was hopelessly lost. It was hot, and his clothes felt heavy, when through the trees he saw a shady pond. Tethering his horse to a tree, he stripped off his clothes and dived into the cool water. He did not see a thin bony hand reaching out of the bushes.

Claude came out of the water refreshed and hungry, but on the bank he found nothing but a coil of rope.

Claude tied some leafy branches around his waist with the rope. Then he ate some of the strawberries that were growing on the bank. Feeling better, he chose a stout branch as a walking stick and set off to find his way home. But as the day drew to a close, Claude realized that he would have to spend the night in the forest.

Peering about in the gloom, he saw before him the entrance to a large cave and felt his way inside. As he grew accustomed to the dark, Claude realized that he was not alone. There seemed to be something with glittering eyes and sharp horns near the mouth of the cave.

⁘

"Stay back! I'm armed!" Claude shouted. But the creature came no closer. Then something moved near the back of the cave. Claude clutched his stick for protection and drew his legs up onto a ledge. He lay there until, exhausted, he fell asleep.

When Claude woke it was morning and a little nanny goat was standing before him, tossing her head. He laughed with relief. It must have been she who had been at the back of the cave in the night.

Claude looked around. A young rooster was pecking busily near a nest full of eggs. A clay jug and a stone ax hung on the wall above Claude's head. Several rough baskets stood on the floor, and there was ash from a recent fire.

"'This is someone's home," thought Claude. "Perhaps I should feed the animals." He gave the hens some grain which he found in a bowl and picked some fresh grass for the goat as a special treat. Then he helped himself to goat's milk and eggs.

The goat nuzzled his hand, and he scratched her behind the ears. She frisked about and followed him when he set off to explore.

Not far away, Claude found a bees' nest in a tree, its honeycomb shining from inside the hollow trunk. Covering his body with mud to protect himself from stings, he climbed up to collect some honey.

Just then, a party of his father's men broke through the trees, blowing their horns and hallooing for him.

"They'll think I've gone mad, if they see me sitting in a tree covered with mud," thought Claude. "I can't let them see me without my clothes and my boots. I would be disgraced!"

So he let the party pass without revealing himself. Then he climbed down from the tree and crept back to the cave, followed all the time by the goat.

"I'll borrow something to cover myself from the owner of the cave when he returns, and then I'll set off for home again," Claude said to his new friend, the goat. But time passed, and no one came. Claude lived on in the cave, growing leaner and stronger every day.

As the warm days went by, Claude forgot altogether about clothes. He nearly forgot that he was Claude, the Squire's son. He became Milker-of-the-Goat, Feeder-of-the-Hens, Friend-of-All-Wild-Animals. The forest creatures were not afraid of him. He fed them, talked to them, and spent hours watching them hunt and play.

As the berries, fruits, and nuts ripened, Claude became Gatherer-and-Preserver. When the grain was harvested in distant fields, he became Gleaner, venturing out at night to gather the leftovers for himself and his animals.

Claude was enjoying his new life. Even the sun and the moon seemed to smile upon him.

One morning, after a heavy rainstorm, Claude heard a frantic bellow coming from the direction of the river. He hurried there to see what was wrong, and found a cow who had been separated from her calf. They had taken shelter from the rain in a hilltop thicket, and as the water rose the river had surrounded them, turning the hillock into an island. The terrified calf would not follow its mother through the swirling current, and the cow was mooing loudly for help.

Claude waded across the water, picked up the calf, and carried it to its mother. Gratefully, the cow licked his hand and then led her calf away through the forest toward the safety of the farmyard.

As the days grew colder, Claude added more ivy leaves to his costume. He tucked strips of moss and lichen between them to keep out the cold. He pounded birch bark to make it soft and sewed pieces together to make a curtain for the mouth of the cave. After several attempts he even succeeded in making himself some birch-bark boots.

He built a fireplace near the entrance. He had found stones the right size and shape to make a mortar and a pestle, and each day he ground grain or nuts or acorns into flour. The smell of baking bread filled the air. A family of hedgehogs moved in.

The cave was now well stocked with food. Strings of mushrooms, parsnips, wild onions, and herbs hung on drying poles. Claude made slings

for the fruit and vegetables he had gathered.
He formed barrels out of bark to hold apples and
roots. Baskets of nuts, grain, and seeds were
stored on a shelf above his mossy bed.

One day when Claude was out gathering
acorns, he encountered a fierce wild boar
threatening two small children from the village.

"Don't be such a selfish swine!" Claude spoke
firmly to the boar. "There are enough acorns
for everyone. Go away and let the children
have their share."

The boar snorted defiantly
but turned and
trotted back
into the
forest.

"There, there, don't cry. The old boar is gone now," Claude comforted the children.

The girl looked up through her tears at the tall, sunburned man. He seemed as ancient, green, and moss-covered as the oak tree that towered above them.

"Are you the Green Man?" she asked in a whisper.

Claude looked down in surprise. Warm sunshine caressed his hair. A gentle breeze rippled his leafy costume. His feet felt as if they were rooted in the earth.

"Yes," Claude answered her at last, "I am the Green Man." He helped the children to gather up their acorns and filled their basket to the brim. Then he led them safely to the edge of the forest.

•••

When winter came, at night Claude visited the
nearby sleeping villages. He helped himself to
some of the food put out for him but always
left some for hungry, prowling animals. At times
he felt lonely as he walked through the deserted
streets, looking into the windows of the cozy
houses. He was homesick for his own village
and his family. But he returned each night to his
cave and his animals. He was needed now in
the forest.

Winter passed and spring was on its way.
The smell of budding leaves, warm earth,
and growing things filled the air. The days went
by, and when he knew that the strawberries
would be ripening by the pond, Claude went
to pick them.

A man was splashing in the water. A fine suit
of clothing lay on the bank and a handsome
horse was tethered nearby.

Claude quietly took off his leaves and put on
the clothes. He found shears and a glass in
the horse's saddlebag, so he cut his long hair
and trimmed his beard. Then he rode through
the forest until he found his own home.

His mother and father were amazed and delighted to see him. Everyone thought that he had been killed long ago by robbers or eaten by wild animals.

"It was the Green Man who saved my life," was all that Claude would say.

His year away had changed the arrogant young man. Now he was hospitable to travelers. He cared for his animals. And each night Claude set out food and drink for the Green Man.

"Do you imagine this is the whole of the world?"

THE UGLY DUCKLING

Hans Christian Andersen

It was so lovely in the country—it was summer! The wheat was yellow, the oats were green, the hay was stacked in the green meadows, and down there the stork went tiptoeing on his red legs, jabbering Egyptian, a language his mother had taught him. Round about the fields and meadows were great forests, and in the midst of those forests lay deep lakes. Yes, it was indeed lovely in the country! Bathed in sunshine there stood an old manor house, surrounded by a deep moat, and from the walls down to the water's edge the bank was covered with great wild rhubarb leaves so high that little children

could stand upright under the biggest of them.
The place was as much of a wilderness as the
densest wood, and there sat a duck on her nest;
she was busy hatching her ducklings, but she
was almost tired of it, because sitting is such
a tedious business, and she had very few callers.
The other ducks thought it more fun to swim
about in the moat than to come and have a
gossip with her under a wild rhubarb leaf.

At last one eggshell after another began to
crack open. "Cheep, cheep!" All the yolks had
come to life and were sticking out their heads.

"Quack, quack," said the duck, and all her
ducklings came scurrying out as fast as they
could, looking about under the green
leaves, and their mother let
them look as much as they
liked, because green
is good for
the eyes.

"How big the world is!" said all the ducklings, for they felt much more comfortable now than when they were lying in the egg.

"Do you imagine this is the whole of the world?" asked their mother. "It goes far beyond the other side of the garden, right into the Rector's field, but I've never been there yet. I hope you're all here," she went on, and hoisted herself up. "No, I haven't got all of you even now; the biggest egg is still there. I wonder how much longer it will take! I'm getting rather bored with the whole thing." And she squatted down again on the nest.

"Well, how are you getting on?" asked an old duck who came to call on her.

"That last egg is taking an awfully long time," said the brooding duck. "It won't break; but let me show you the others, they're the sweetest ducklings I've ever seen. They are all exactly like their father; the scamp—he never comes to see me!"

"Let me look at the egg that won't break," said the old duck. "You may be sure it's a turkey's egg. I was fooled like that once, and the trouble and bother I had with those youngsters, because they were actually afraid of the water! I simply couldn't get them to go in! I quacked at them and I snapped at them, but it was no use. Let me see the egg—of course it's a turkey's egg. Leave it alone, and teach the other children to swim."

"Oh, well, if I've taken so much trouble I may just as well sit a little longer," said the duck.

"Please yourself," said the old duck, and she waddled off.

At last the big egg cracked. "Cheep, cheep!" said the youngster, scrambling out; he was so big and ugly! The duck looked at him: "What a frightfully big duckling that one is," she said. "None of the others looked like that! Could he possibly be a turkey chick? We'll soon find out; he'll have to go into the water, even if I have to kick him in myself!"

The next day the weather was simply glorious; the sun shone on all the wild rhubarb plants. Mother Duck appeared with her family down by the moat. Splash! There she was in the water!

"Quack, quack," she said, and one duckling after another plumped in. The water closed over their heads, but they were up again in a second and floated beautifully. Their legs worked of their own accord; they were all out in the water now, and even the ugly gray creature was swimming along with them.

"That's no turkey!" she said. "Look how nicely he uses his legs, and how straight he holds himself! He's my own flesh and blood, I tell you. He isn't really so bad when you take a good look at him. Quack, quack—come along with me, I'll bring you out into the world and introduce you to the duckyard, but keep close to me or you may get stepped on, and look out for the cat!"

So they made their entrance into the duckyard. What a pandemonium there was! Two families were quarreling over an eel's head; but in the end the cat got it.

"There you are, that's the way of the world!"
said Mother Duck, licking her lips, for she did so
want the eel's head herself. "Now use your
legs," she said. "Move about briskly and
curtsey with your necks to the old duck
over there; she is the most aristocratic
person here, and of Spanish blood,
that's why she is so stout; and be
sure to observe that red rag round
her leg. It's a great distinction, and
the highest honor that can be
bestowed upon a duck; it means
that her owner wishes to keep her,
and that she is to be specially noticed by
man and beast. Now hurry! Don't turn your
toes in; a well-brought-up duckling turns
his toes out just as father and mother
do—like that. That's right! Now
make a deep curtsey with your
necks and say, 'Quack, quack!'"

And they did as they were told; but
the other ducks all round about looked at them
and said out loud, "There now! Have we got to
have that crowd too? As if there weren't enough
of us already; and ugh, what a dreadful-looking
creature that duckling is! We won't put up

with him." And immediately a duck rushed at him and bit him in the neck.

"Leave him alone," said the mother. "He's not bothering any of you."

"I know," said the duck who had bitten him, "but he's too big and odd. What he wants is a good smacking."

"Those are pretty children you've got, Mother," said the old duck with the rag round her leg. "They are all nice-looking except that one—he didn't turn out so well. I wish he could be made all over again!"

"That can't be done, Your Grace," said Mother Duck. "He's not handsome, but he's as good as gold, and he swims as well as any of the others, I daresay even a little better. I expect his looks will improve, or perhaps in time his size won't be so noticeable. He was in the egg too long, that's why he isn't properly shaped." And she pecked his neck and brushed up the little man. "As it happens he's a drake," she added, "so it doesn't matter quite so much.

I think he'll be a strong fellow, and I'm sure he'll make his mark in the world."

"The other ducklings are lovely," said the old duck. "Make yourselves at home, and if you find an eel's head—you may bring it to me."

So at once they felt at home.

But the poor duckling who was the last to be hatched, and who looked so ugly, was bitten and buffeted about and made fun of both by the ducks and the hens. "He's too big!" they all said. And the turkey-cock, who was born with spurs and consequently thought he was an emperor, blew himself up like a ship in full sail and made for him, gobbling and gabbling till his wattles were quite purple. The poor duckling did not know where to turn; he was so miserable because of his ugliness and because he was the butt of the whole barnyard.

And so it went on all the first day, and after that matters grew worse and worse. The poor duckling was chased about by everyone; his own brothers and sisters were downright nasty to him and always said, "I hope the cat gets you, you skinny bag of bones!" And even his mother said, "I wish you were miles away!" And the ducks bit him and the hens pecked him, and the girl who fed them kicked him with her foot.

So, half running and half flying, he got over the fence.

The little birds in the bushes rose up in alarm. "That's because I'm so ugly," thought the duckling, and closed his eyes, but he kept on running and finally came out into the great marsh where the wild ducks lived. There he lay the whole night long, tired and downhearted.

In the morning the wild ducks flew up and looked at their new companion. "What sort of a fellow are you?" they asked, and the duckling turned in all directions, bowing to everybody as nicely as he could.

"You're appallingly ugly!" said the wild ducks. "But why should we care so long as you don't marry into our family?" Poor thing! As if he had any thought of marrying! All he wanted to do was to lie among the reeds and drink a little marsh water.

So he lay there for two
whole days, and then
came two wild geese, or
rather ganders, for they
were two young men;
they had not been out
of the egg very long,
and that was why
they were so cocky.

"Listen, young
fellow," they said,
"you're so ugly that we
quite like you. Will you
join us and be a bird of
passage? Close by, in another
marsh, there are some lovely
wild geese, all nice young girls,
and they can all say 'Quack.' You're
so ugly that you might appeal to them."

Two shots rang out—bang! bang!—both
ganders fell dead among the reeds, and the water
was reddened with their blood. Bang! bang! was
heard again, and whole flocks of wild geese flew
up from the reeds, and—bang! bang! bang! again
and again. A great shoot was going on. The men

94

were lying under cover all round the marsh, and some of them were even up in the trees whose branches stretched out above the reeds. Blue smoke drifted in among the dark trees and was carried far out over the water. Through the mud came the gun-dogs—splash! splash!—bending down the reeds and rushes on every side. The poor duckling was scared out of his wits, and tried to hide his head under his wing, when suddenly a fierce-looking dog came close to him, with his tongue hanging far out of his mouth and his wild eyes gleaming horribly. He opened his jaws wide, showed his sharp teeth, and—splash! splash!—off he went without touching the duckling.

"Thank heaven!" he sighed. "I'm so ugly that even the dog won't bother to bite me!"

And so he lay perfectly still, while the shots rattled through the reeds as gun after gun was fired.

It was toward evening when everything quieted down, but the poor duckling dared not

stir yet. He waited several hours before he
looked about him, and then hurried away from
the marsh as fast as he could. He ran over
field and meadow, hardly able to fight
against the strong wind.

Late that night he reached a wretched little
hut, so wretched, in fact, that it did not
know which way to fall, and that
is why it remained standing
upright. The wind whistled
so fiercely round the
duckling that the
poor thing simply
had to sit down on
his little tail to resist it.

The storm grew worse and
worse. Then he noticed that the door had
come off one of its hinges and hung so crooked
that he could slip into the room through the
opening, and that is what he did.

An old woman lived here with her tomcat and
her hen. The cat, whom she called "Sonny,"
knew how to arch his back and purr; in fact he
could even give out sparks, but for that you
had to rub his fur the wrong way. The hen had
little short legs and was called "Stumpy."

She was an excellent layer and the old woman loved her as her own child.

Next morning they at once noticed the strange duckling; the cat began to purr and the hen to cluck.

"What's the matter?" asked the old woman, looking about her; but her eyes were not very good, and so she mistook the duckling for a fat duck that had lost her way. "What a windfall!" she said. "Now I shall have duck's eggs—if it doesn't happen to be a drake. We must make sure of that." So the duckling was taken on trial for three weeks, but not a single egg came along.

Now the cat was master of the house, and the hen was mistress, and they always said, "We, and the world"; for they imagined themselves to be not only half the world, but by far the better half. The duckling thought that other people might be allowed to have an opinion too, but the hen could not see that at all.

"Can you lay eggs?" she asked.

"No."

"Well, then, you'd better keep your mouth shut!"

＊＊＊

And the cat said, "Can you arch your back, purr, and give out sparks?"

"No."

"Well, then, you can't have any opinion worth offering when sensible people are speaking."

The duckling sat in a corner, feeling very gloomy and depressed. Then he suddenly thought of the fresh air and the bright sunshine, and such a longing came over him to swim in the water that he could not help telling the hen about it.

"What's the matter with you?" asked the hen. "You haven't got anything to do, that's why you get these silly ideas. Either lay eggs or purr and you'll soon be all right."

"But it's so delightful to swim in the water," said the duckling, "so delightful to get it over your head and dive down to the bottom!"

"Yes, it must be delightful!" said the hen. "You've gone crazy, I think. Ask the cat, the cleverest creature I know, if he likes swimming or diving. I say nothing of myself. Ask our mistress, the old woman, as well; no one in the world is wiser than she. Do you think she would like to swim or to get the water over her head?"

"You don't understand me," said the duckling.

"Well, if we don't understand you, then who would? You surely don't imagine you're wiser than the cat or the old woman?—not to mention myself, of course. Don't give yourself such airs, child, but be grateful to your Maker for all the kindness you have received. Didn't you get into a warm room, and haven't you fallen in with people who can teach you a thing or two? But you talk such nonsense, it's no fun at all to have you about. Believe me, I wish you well. I tell you unpleasant things, but that's the way to know one's real friends. Come on, hurry up, see that you lay eggs, and do learn how to purr or to give out sparks!"

"I think I had better go out into the wide world," said the duckling.

"Please yourself," said the hen.

So the duckling went away: he swam in the water and dived down into it, but he was still snubbed by every creature because of his ugliness.

Autumn set in. The leaves in the woods turned yellow and brown: the wind caught them and whirled them about; up in the air it looked very cold. The clouds hung low, heavy with hail and snowflakes, and on the fence perched the raven, trembling with the cold and croaking, "Caw! Caw!" The mere thought of it was enough to make anybody shiver. The poor duckling was certainly to be pitied!

One evening, when the sun was setting in all its splendor, a large flock of big handsome birds came out of the bushes. The duckling had never before seen anything quite so beautiful as these birds. They were dazzlingly white, with long supple necks—they were swans! They uttered a most uncanny cry and spread their splendid great wings to fly away from the cold regions, away to warmer countries, to open lakes. They rose so high, so very high in the air, that a strange feeling came over the ugly little duckling as he watched them. He turned round

and round in
the water like a wheel, craned his
neck to follow their flight, and uttered a cry
so loud and strange that it frightened him.

He could not forget those noble birds, those
happy birds, and when they were lost to sight
he dived down to the bottom of the water; then
when he came up again he was quite beside
himself. He did not know what the birds were
called, nor where they were flying to, and yet he
loved them more than he had ever loved
anything. He did not envy them in the least; it
would never have occurred to him to want such
beauty for himself. He would have been quite
content if only the ducks would have put up
with him—the poor ugly creature!

And the winter grew so cold, so bitterly cold. The duckling was forced to swim about in the water to keep it from freezing altogether, but every night the opening became smaller and smaller; at last it froze so hard that the ice made cracking noises, and the duckling had to keep on paddling to prevent the opening from closing up. In the end he was exhausted and lay quite still, caught in the ice.

Early next morning a farmer came by, and when he saw him he went onto the ice, broke it with his wooden shoe, and carried him home to his wife. There the duckling revived.

The children wanted to play with him, but he thought they meant to do him harm, so he fluttered, terrified, into the milk pail, splashing the milk all over the room. The woman screamed and threw up her hands in fright. Then he flew into the butter tub, and from that into the flour barrel and out again. What a sight he was! The woman shrieked and struck at him with the tongs. Laughing and shouting, the children fell over each other trying to catch him. Fortunately the door was open, so the duckling dashed out into the bushes and lay there in the newly fallen snow, as if in a daze.

It would be too sad, however, to tell all the trouble and misery he had to suffer during that cruel winter. . . . When the sun began to shine warmly he found himself once more in the marsh among the reeds. The larks were singing—it was spring, beautiful spring!

Then suddenly he spread his wings; the sound of their whirring made him realize how much stronger they had grown, and they carried him powerfully along. Before he knew it, he found himself in a great garden where the apple trees stood in bloom, and the lilac filled the air with its fragrance, bending down the long green branches over the meandering streams.

It was so lovely here, so full of the freshness of spring. And look! From out of the thicket in front of him came three beautiful white swans. They ruffled their feathers proudly and floated so lightly on the water. The duckling recognized the glorious creatures and felt a strange sadness come over him.

"I will fly near those royal birds, and they will peck me to death for daring to bring my ugly self near them. But that doesn't matter in the least! Better to be killed by them than to be bitten by the ducks, pecked by the hens, kicked by the girl in charge of the hen-run, and suffer untold agony in winter."

···

Then he flew into the water and swam toward the beautiful swans. They saw him and dashed at him with outspread rustling feathers. "Kill me," said the poor creature, and he bowed his head down upon the surface of the stream, expecting death. But what was this he saw mirrored in the clear water? He saw beneath him his own image, but it was no longer the image of an awkward dirty gray bird, ugly and repulsive— he himself was a swan!

It does not matter being born in a duckyard, if only one has lain in a swan's egg.

He felt quite glad to have been through so much trouble and adversity, for now he could fully appreciate not only his own good fortune, but also all the beauty that greeted him. The great swans swam round him and stroked him with their beaks.

Some little children came to the garden to throw bread and corn into the water, and the youngest exclaimed, "There's a new one!" And the other children chimed in, "Yes, there's a new one!" They clapped their hands, danced about, and ran to fetch their father and mother.

Bread and cake were thrown into the water, and everyone said, "The new one is the most beautiful of all! He's so young and handsome!" And the old swans bowed to him.

That made him feel quite embarrassed, and he put his head under his wing, not knowing what it was all about. An overwhelming happiness filled him, and yet he was not at all proud, for a good heart never becomes proud.

He remembered how once he had been despised and persecuted; and now he heard

everyone saying that he was the most beautiful of all beautiful birds.

And the lilac bushes dipped their branches into the water before him; and the sun shone warm and mild. He rustled his feathers and held his graceful neck high, and from the depths of his heart he joyfully exclaimed, "I never dreamt that so much happiness was possible when I was the ugly duckling."

He knew she was a moon goddess.

WHITE WAVE

Chinese folktale
as told by Diane Wolkstein

In the hills of southern China, there once stood a
shrine. It was made of stones—beautiful white,
pink, and gray stones—and was built as a house
for a goddess.

Now the stones lie scattered on the hillside. If
you should happen to find one, remember this
story . . . of the stones, the shrine, and the goddess
White Wave.

Long ago, in the time of mysteries, a young
farmer was walking home from the fields in the
evening. He walked slowly, for he was not eager

to return to his house. He lived alone. His parents had died two years before. He was too poor to marry and too shy to speak with any of the young women in his village.

As he passed through a small forest, he saw a stone, a beautiful white stone, gleaming in the moonlight.

The young man, whose name was Kuo Ming, bent over to look at the stone. It wasn't white. It was every color in the rainbow. And when he held it in his hands, he saw it wasn't a stone at all but a snail, a moon snail. And what was the most wonderful good fortune—it was alive!

The farmer gently carried the snail home and placed it in an earthenware jar. Then, before fixing his own dinner, he went out again and gathered fresh leaves for the snail.

The first thing he did the next morning was to look in the jar. The leaves were gone. The

snail had eaten them. Kuo Ming picked four
more leaves and went off to the fields to work.

When he came home that evening, the farmer
found his dinner waiting for him on the table—a
bowl of cooked rice, steamed vegetables, and a
cup of hot tea.

He looked around the room. No one was
there. He went to the door and looked out into
the night. No one. He left the door open, hoping
that whoever had prepared his dinner might
join him.

The next evening, his dinner was again
waiting for him—and this time there was a
branch of wild peach set in a vase on the table.
The farmer made a special trip to the village to
ask if strangers had arrived. No one knew of any.

Every morning, he left leaves for the snail. Every evening, his dinner was waiting, and always there was a wildflower in the vase.

One morning, Kuo Ming woke up earlier than usual. He took his rake and started off as if he were going to the fields. Instead he circled back to his house and stood outside the window, listening. There was no sound. Then, as the first light of the day touched the earth, he heard a noise.

He looked in the window and saw a tiny white hand rising from the jar. It rose higher and higher. Then a second white hand rose from the jar and out leaped a beautiful girl.

She was pure light. Her dress was made of silk, and as she moved, her dress rippled, changing from silver to white to gold. Wherever she stepped in the room, the room shone.

He knew, though no one had told him, that she was a moon goddess. And he knew, though no one had told him, that he must never try to touch her.

The next morning, before he went to work, he watched her, and the next morning, and the next.

As the days went by, his loneliness disappeared. He skipped to the fields in the morning and walked quickly home in the evening. His dinner was always waiting. The house was shining. The air was sweet. And his heart was full.

Many days passed. Then, one morning, as he was watching her sweep the floor, her long black hair fell across her face, and a great longing came upon him. He wanted to touch her hair. The desire burst upon him so strongly and quickly that he forgot what he knew. He opened the door and rushed into the room.

"Do not move," she said.

"Who are you?" he asked.

"I am White Wave, the moon goddess. But now I must leave you, for you have forgotten what you knew."

"No!" he cried.

"Good farmer," she said, "if you can hold yourself still and count for me, I will leave you a gift. Let me hear you count. Count to five."

"One," he whispered.

She crossed in front of him and walked toward the open door.

"Two," he said softly.

"I leave you my shell."

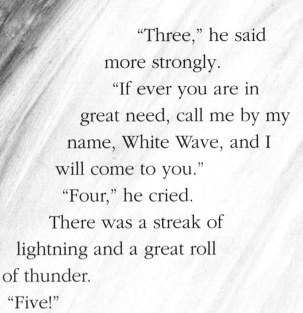

"Three," he said
more strongly.

"If ever you are in
great need, call me by my
name, White Wave, and I
will come to you."

"Four," he cried.

There was a streak of
lightning and a great roll
of thunder.

"Five!"

A huge wind came and swept the
goddess into the air. He ran outside, but
the rain poured down so fast that he could
not see her.

He stood in the pouring rain a long time.
Then he went back into the house. The snail
shell was there. He picked it up. No living
creature was inside.

Kuo Ming went to the fields, but he did not
think of his work. He thought only of White
Wave and how to bring her back.

As he was wandering over the hills, his foot
struck a stone. He bent over to look at it. At that
moment, he decided he would build a shrine for
White Wave—a beautiful stone house where she

might live peacefully. He spent more time choosing the stones—beautiful white, pink, and gray stones—than working in the fields. When the harvest came, it was very small. He ate the little there was. He ate the supplies he had stored, and after that he lived on berries and wild grass.

At last, one evening, the shrine was complete. But that evening the farmer was so weak with hunger, he could barely walk. He stumbled into his house and tripped over the earthenware jar. The shell fell out.

Quickly he picked it up, and as he held it, he remembered the words of the goddess: "If ever you are in great need, call me by my name, White Wave . . ."

The farmer held the shell in front of him. Then he raised it in the air, and with his last strength he cried: *White Wave, I need you.*

Slowly he turned the shell toward him. A wave of gleaming white rice cascaded out of the shell and onto the floor. He dipped his hands into it. The rice was solid and firm. It was enough to last him until the next harvest.

He never called her name again. With the flowing of the rice, a new strength had come to him. Kuo Ming worked hard in the fields. The rice grew. The vegetables flourished. He married and had children. But he did not forget White Wave.

He told his wife about her, and when his children were old enough, he took them on his knee and told them the story of White Wave. The children liked to hold the shell in their hands as they listened to the story.

The shrine stood on the hill above their house. The children often went there in the early morning and evening, hoping to see White Wave. They never did.

When the old man died, the shell was lost. In time the shrine, too, disappeared. All that remained was the story.

But that is how it is with all of us: when we die, all that remains is the story.

"What is fly?" asked the mousewife.

THE MOUSEWIFE

Rumer Godden

Wherever there is an old house with wooden floors and beams and rafters and wooden stairs and wainscots and skirting boards and larders, there are mice. They creep out on the carpets for crumbs, they whisk in and out of their holes, they run in the wainscot and between the ceiling and the floors. There are no signposts because they know the way, and no milestones because no one is there to see how they run.

In the old nursery rhyme, when the cat went to see the queen, he caught a little mouse under her chair; that was long long ago and

that queen was different from our queen,
but the mouse was the same.

Mice have always been the same. There
are no fashions in mice, they do not change.
If a mouse could have a portrait painted
of his great-great-grandfather, and *his* great-
grandfather, it would be the portrait of a
mouse today.

But once there was a little mousewife who
was different from the rest.

She looked the same; she had the same ears
and prick nose and whiskers and dewdrop
eyes; the same little bones and grey fur;
the same skinny paws and long skinny tail.

She did all the things a mousewife does: she made a nest for the mouse babies she hoped to have one day; she collected crumbs of food for her husband and herself; once she bit the tops off a whole bowl of crocuses; and she played with the other mice at midnight on the attic floor.

"What more do you want?" asked her husband.

She did not know what it was she wanted, but she wanted more.

The house where these mice lived belonged to a spinster lady called Miss Barbara Wilkinson. The mice thought the house was the whole world. The garden and the wood that lay round it were as far away to them as the stars are to you, but the mousewife used sometimes to creep up on the windowsill and press her whiskers close against the pane.

In spring she saw snowdrops and appleblossom in the garden and bluebells in the wood; in summer there were roses; in autumn all the trees changed colour; and in winter they were bare until the snow came and they were white with snow.

The mousewife saw all these through the windowpane, but she did not know what they were.

She was a house mouse, not a garden mouse
or a field mouse; she could not go outside.

"I think about cheese," said her husband.
"Why don't you think about cheese?"

Then, at Christmas, he had an attack of
indigestion through eating rich crumbs of
Christmas cake. "There were currants in those
crumbs," said the mousewife. "They have upset
you. You must go to bed and be kept warm."
She decided to move the mousehole to a space
behind the fender where it was warm. She lined
the new hole with tufts of carpet wool and

put her husband to bed wrapped in a pattern of grey flannel that Miss Wilkinson's lazy maid, Flora, had left in the dustpan. "But I am grateful to Flora," said the mousewife's husband as he settled himself comfortably in bed.

Now the mousewife had to find all the food for the family in addition to keeping the hole swept and clean.

She had no time for thinking.

While she was busy, a boy brought a dove to Miss Wilkinson. He had caught it in the wood. It was a pretty thing, a turtledove. Miss Wilkinson put it in a cage on the ledge of her sitting-room window.

The cage was an elegant one; it had gilt bars and a door that opened if its catch were pressed down; there were small gilt trays for water and peas. Miss Wilkinson hung up a lump of sugar and a piece of fat. "There, you have everything you want," said Miss Barbara Wilkinson.

For a day or two the dove pecked at the bars and opened and shut its wings. Sometimes it called "Roo coo, roo coo," then it was silent.

"Why won't it eat?" asked Miss Barbara Wilkinson. "Those are the very best peas."

A mouse family seldom has enough to eat. It is difficult to come by crumbs, especially in such a neat, tidy house as Miss Barbara Wilkinson's. It was the peas that first attracted the attention of the mousewife to the cage when at last she had time to go up on the windowsill. "I have been running here and there and everywhere to get us food," she said, "not allowing myself to come up onto the windowsill, and here are these fine white peas, not to mention this piece of fat." (She did not care for the sugar.)

She squeezed through the bars of the cage but, as she was taking the first pea from the tray, the dove moved its wings. I cannot tell you

how quickly the mousewife pressed herself back through the bars and jumped down from the sill and ran across the floor and whisked into her hole. It was quicker than a cat can wink its eye. (She thought it was the cat.)

In spite of her great fright she could not help thinking of those peas. She was very hungry.

"I had better not go back," she said. "There is something dangerous there," but back she went the very next day.

Soon the dove grew quite used to the mousewife going in and out, and the mouse grew quite used to the dove.

"This is better," said Miss Barbara Wilkinson. "The dove is eating its peas," but, of course, he was not; it was the mouse.

The dove kept his wings folded. The mousewife thought him large and strange and ugly with the speckles on his breast and his fine down. (She thought of it as fur, not feathers.) He was not at all like a mouse; his voice was deep and soft, quite unlike hers, which was a small, high squeaking. Most strange of all, to her, was that he let her take his peas; when she offered them to him he turned his head aside on his breast.

"Then at least take a little water," begged the mousewife, but he said he did not like water. "Only dew, dew, dew," he said.

"What is dew?" asked the mousewife.

He could not tell her what dew was, but he told her how it shines on the leaves and grass in the early morning for doves to drink. That made him think of night in the woods and of how he and his mate would come down with the first light to walk on the wet earth and peck for food, and of how, then, they would fly over the fields to other woods farther away. He told this to the mousewife too.

"What is fly?" asked the ignorant little mousewife.

"Don't you know?" asked the dove in surprise. He stretched out his wings and they hit the cage bars. Still he struggled to spread them, but the bars were too close, and he sank back on his perch and sank his head on his breast.

The mousewife was strangely moved but she did not know why.

Because he would not eat his peas she brought him crumbs of bread and, once, a preserved blackberry that had fallen from

a tart. (But he would not eat the blackberry.)
Every day he talked to her about the world
outside the window.

He told her of roofs and the tops of trees and
of the rounded shapes of hills and the flat look
of fields and of the mountains far away. "But I
have never flown as far as that," he said, and he
was quiet. He was thinking now he never would.

To cheer him the mousewife asked him to
tell her about the wind; she heard it in the
house on stormy nights, shaking the doors and
windows with more noise than all the mice
put together. The dove told her how it blew in
the cornfields, making patterns in the corn,

127

and of how it made different sounds in the different sorts of trees, and of how it blew up the clouds and sent them across the sky.

He told her these things as a dove would see them, as it flew, and the mousewife, who was used to creeping, felt her head growing dizzy as if she were spinning on her tail, but all she said was, "Tell me more."

Each day the dove told her more. When she came he would lift his head and call to her, "Roo coo, roo coo," in his most gentle voice.

"Why do you spend so much time on the windowsill?" asked her husband. "I do not like it. The proper place for a mousewife is in her hole or coming out for crumbs and frolic with me."

The mousewife did not answer. She looked far away.

Then, on a happy day, she had a nestful of baby mice. They were not as big as half your thumb, and they were pink and hairless, with pink shut eyes and little pink tails like threads. The mousewife loved them very much. The eldest, who was a girl, she called Flannelette, after the pattern of grey flannel.

For several days she thought of nothing and no
one else. She was also busy with her husband.
His digestion was no better.

One afternoon he went over to the opposite
wall to see a friend. He was well enough to do
that, he said, but certainly not well enough to go
out and look for crumbs. The mice-babies were
asleep, the hole was quiet, and the mousewife
began to think of the dove. Presently she tucked
the nest up carefully and went up on the
windowsill to see him; also she was hungry
and needed some peas.

What a state he was in! He was drooping and
nearly exhausted because he had eaten scarcely

anything while she had been away. He cowered over her with his wings and kissed her with his beak; she had not known his feathers were so soft or that his breast was so warm. "I thought you had gone, gone, gone," he said over and over again.

"Tut! Tut!" said the mousewife. "A body has other things to do. I can't be always running off to you." But, though she pretended to scold him, she had a tear at the end of her whisker for the poor dove. (Mouse tears look like millet seeds, which are the smallest seeds I know.)

She stayed a long time with the dove. When she went home, I am sorry to say, her husband bit her on the ear.

That night she lay awake thinking of the dove; mice stay up a great part of the night, but, towards dawn, they, too, curl into their beds and sleep. The mousewife could not sleep. She still thought of the dove. "I cannot visit him as much as I could wish," she said. "There is my husband, and he has never bitten me before. There are the children, and it is surprising how quickly crumbs are eaten up. And no one would believe how dirty a hole can get if it is not attended to every day. But that is not the worst of it. The dove should not be in that cage. It is thoughtless of Miss Barbara Wilkinson." She grew angry as she thought of it. "Not to be able to scamper about the floor! Not to be able to run in and out, or climb up the larder to get at the cheese! Not to flick in and out and to whisk and to feel how you run in your tail! To sit in the trap until your little bones are stiff and your whiskers grow stupid because there is nothing for them to smell or hear or see!" The mousewife could only think of it as a mouse, but she could feel as the dove could feel.

Her husband and Flannelette and the other children were breathing and squeaking happily in their sleep, but the mousewife could hear her heart beating; the beats were little, like the tick of a watch, but they felt loud and disturbing to her. "I cannot sleep," said the mousewife, and then, suddenly, she felt she must go then, that minute, to the dove. "It is too late. He will be asleep," she said, but still she felt she should go.

She crept from her bed and out of the hole onto the floor by the fender. It was bright moonlight, so bright that it made her blink.

• • •

It was bright as day, but a strange day, that
made her head swim and her tail tremble.
Her whiskers quivered this way and that, but
there was no one and nothing to be seen;
no sound, no movement anywhere.

She crept across the pattern of the carpet,
stopping here and there on a rose or a leaf or on
the scroll of the border. At last she reached the
wall and ran lightly up onto the windowsill
and looked into the cage. In the moonlight she
could see the dove sleeping in his feathers,
which were ruffled up so that he looked plump
and peaceful, but, as she watched, he dreamed

and called "roo coo" in his sleep and shivered
as if he moved. "He is dreaming of scampering
and running free," said the mousewife.
"Poor thing! Poor dove!"

She looked out into the garden. It too was
as bright as day, but the same strange day.
She could see the tops of the trees in the wood,
and she knew, all at once, that was where
the dove should be, in the trees and the garden
and the wood.

He called "roo coo" again in his sleep—and
she saw that the window was open.

Her whiskers grew still and then they
stiffened. She thought of the catch on the cage
door. If the catch were pressed down, the
door opened.

"I shall open it," said the mousewife. "I shall
jump on it and hang from it and swing from it,
and it will be pressed down; the door will
open and the dove can come out. He can whisk
quite out of sight. Miss Barbara Wilkinson will
not be able to catch him."

She jumped at the cage and caught the catch
in her strong little teeth and swung. The door
sprang open, waking the dove.

He was startled and lifted his wings and
they hit hard against the cage so that it shivered
and the mousewife was almost shaken off.

"Hurry! Hurry!" she said through her teeth.

In a heavy sidelong way he sidled to the door
and stood there looking. The mousewife would
have given him a push, but she was holding
down the catch.

At the door of the cage the dove stretched his
neck towards the open window. "Why does he
not hurry?" thought the mousewife. "I cannot stay
here much longer. My teeth are cracking."

He did not see her or look towards her;
then—clap—he took her breath away so that she

fell. He had opened his wings and flown straight
out. For a moment he dipped as if he would
fall, his wings were cramped, and then he moved
them and lifted up and up and flew away
across the tops of the trees.

The mousewife picked herself up and shook
out her bones and her fur.

"So that is to fly," she said. "Now I know."
She stood looking out of the window where the
dove had gone.

"He has flown," she said. "Now there is no
one to tell me about the hills and the corn
and the clouds. I shall forget them. How shall
I remember when there is no one to tell me
and there are so many children and crumbs and
bits of fluff to think of?" She had millet tears,
not on her whiskers but in her eyes.

"Tut! tut!" said the mousewife and blinked
them away. She looked out again and saw
the stars.

It has been given to few mice to see the stars;
so rare is it that the mousewife had not even
heard of them, and when she saw them shining
she thought at first they must be new brass
buttons. Then she saw they were very far off,

farther than the garden or the wood, beyond
the farthest trees. "But not too far for me to see,"
she said. She knew now that they were not
buttons but something far and big and strange.
"But not so strange to me," she said, "for I have
seen them. And I have seen them for myself,"
said the mousewife, "without the dove. I can
see for myself," said the mousewife, and slowly,
proudly, she walked back to bed.

She was back in the hole before her husband
woke up, and he did not know that she had
been away.

Miss Barbara Wilkinson was astonished to
find the cage empty next morning and the
dove gone. "Who could have let it out?" asked

136

Miss Wilkinson. She suspected Flora and never knew that she was looking at someone too large and that it was a very small person indeed.

The mousewife is a very old lady mouse now. Her whiskers are grey and she cannot scamper anymore; even her running is slow. But her great-great-grandchildren, the children of the children of the children of Flannelette and Flannelette's brothers and sisters, treat her with the utmost respect.

She is a little different from them, though she looks the same. I think she knows something they do not.

HOW THE TORTOISE BECAME

Ted Hughes

Long ago when the world was brand new, before animals or birds, the sun rose into the sky and brought the first day.

The flowers jumped up and stared round astonished. Then from every side, from under leaves and from behind rocks, creatures began to appear.

In those days the colours were much better than they are now, much brighter. And the air sparkled because it had never been used.

But don't think everything was so easy.

•••

To begin with, all the creatures were pretty much alike—very different from what they are now. They had no idea what they were going to become. Some wanted to become linnets, some wanted to become lions, some wanted to become other things. The ones that wanted to become lions practised at being lions—and by and by, sure enough, they began to turn into lions. So, the ones that wanted to become linnets practised at being linnets, and slowly they turned into linnets. And so on.

But there were other creatures that came about in other ways. . . .

When God made a creature, he first of all shaped it in clay. Then he baked it in the ovens of the sun until it was hard. Then he took it out of the oven and, when it was cool, breathed life into it. Last of all, he pulled its skin onto it like a tight jersey.

All the animals got different skins. If it was a cold day, God would give to the animals he made on that day a dense, woolly skin. Snow was falling heavily when he made the sheep and the bears.

...

If it was a hot day, the new animals got a thin skin. On the day he made greyhounds and dachshunds and boys and girls, the weather was so hot God had to wear a sun hat and was calling endlessly for iced drinks.

Now on the day he made Torto, God was so hot the sweat was running down onto the tips of his fingers.

After baking Torto in the oven, God took him out to cool. Then he flopped back in his chair and ordered Elephant to fan him with its ears. He had made Elephant only a few days before and was very pleased with its big flapping ears. At last he thought that Torto must surely be cool.

"He's had as long as I usually give a little thing like him," he said, and picking up Torto, he breathed life into him. As he did so, he found out his mistake.

Torto was not cool. Far from it. On that hot day, with no cooling breezes, Torto had remained scorching hot. Just as he was when he came out of the oven.

"Ow!" roared God. He dropped Torto and went hopping away on one leg to the other end of his workshop, shaking his burnt fingers.

"Ow, ow, ow!" he roared again, and plunged his hand into a dish of butter to cure the burns.

Torto meanwhile lay on the floor, just alive, groaning with the heat.

"Oh, I'm so hot!" he moaned. "So hot! The heat. Oh, the heat!"

God was alarmed that he had given Torto life before he was properly cooled.

"Just a minute, Torto," he said, "I'll have a nice, thin, cooling skin on you in a jiffy. Then you'll feel better."

•••

But Torto wanted no skin. He was too hot as it was.

"No, no!" he cried. "I shall stifle. Let me go without a skin for a few days. Let me cool off first."

"That's impossible," said God. "All creatures must have skins."

"No, no!" cried Torto, wiping the sweat from his little brow. "No skin!"

"Yes!" cried God.

"No!" cried Torto.

"Yes!"

"No!"

God made a grab at Torto, who ducked and ran like lightning under a cupboard. Without any skin to cumber his movements, Torto felt very light and agile.

"Come out!" roared God, and got down on his knees to grope under the cupboard for Torto.

In a flash, Torto was out from under the other end of the cupboard, and while God was still struggling to his feet, he ran out through the door and into the world, without a skin.

The first thing he did was to go to a cool pond and plunge straight into it. There he lay, for several days, just cooling off. Then he came out and began to live among the other creatures. But he was still very hot. Whenever he felt his own heat getting too much for him, he retired to his pond to cool off in the water. In this way, he found life pleasant enough.

Except for one thing. The other creatures didn't approve of Torto.

They all had skins. When they saw Torto without a skin, they were horrified.

"But he has no skin!" cried Porcupine.

"It's disgusting!" cried Yak. "It's indecent!"

"He's not normal. Leave him to himself," said Sloth.

So all the animals began to ignore Torto. But they couldn't ignore him completely, because he was a wonderfully swift runner, and whenever they held a race, he won it. He was so nimble without a skin that none of the other creatures could hope to keep up with him.

"I'm a genius runner," he said. "You should respect me. I am faster than the lot of you put together. I was made different."

But the animals still ignored him. Even when they had to give him the prizes for winning all the races, they still ignored him.

"Torto is a very swift mover," they said. "And perhaps swifter than any of us. But what sort of a creature is he? No skin!"

And they all turned up their noses.

At first, Torto didn't care at all. When the animals collected together, with all their fur brushed and combed and set neatly, he strolled among them, smiling happily, naked.

"When will this disgusting creature learn to behave?" cried Turkey, loudly enough for everyone to hear.

•••

"Just take no notice of him," said Alligator,
and lumbered round, in his heavy armour,
to face in the opposite direction.

All the animals turned round to face in the
opposite direction.

When Torto went up to Grizzly Bear to ask
what everyone was looking at, Grizzly Bear
pretended to have a fly in his ear. When he went
to Armadillo, Armadillo gathered up all his
sons and daughters and led them off without
a word or a look.

"So that's your game, is it?" said Torto to
himself. Then aloud, he said, "Never mind.
Wait till it comes to the races."

When the races came,
later in the afternoon,
Torto won them all.
But nobody cheered.
He collected the
prizes and went off
to his pond alone.

"They're jealous
of me," he said.
"That's why
they ignore me.

···

But I'll punish them: I'll go on winning all the races."

That night, God came to Torto and begged him to take a proper skin before it was too late. Torto shook his head:

"The other animals are snobs," he said. "Just because they are covered with a skin, they think everyone else should be covered with one too. That's snobbery. But I shall teach them not to be snobs by making them respect me. I shall go on winning all the races."

And so he did. But still the animals didn't respect him. In fact, they grew to dislike him more and more.

One day there was a very important race meeting, and all the animals collected at the usual place. But the minute Torto arrived they simply walked away. Simply got up and walked away. Torto sat on the racetrack and stared after them. He felt really left out.

"Perhaps," he thought sadly, "it would be better if I had a skin. I mightn't be able to run then, but at least I would have friends. I have no friends. Besides, after all this practise, I would still be able to run quite fast."

But as soon as he said that he felt angry with himself.

"No!" he cried. "They are snobs. I shall go on winning their races in spite of them. I shall teach them a lesson."

And he got up from where he was sitting and followed them. He found them all in one place, under a tree. And the races were being run.

"Hey!" he called as he came up to them. "What about me?"

But at that moment, Tiger held up a sign in front of him. On the sign, Torto read: "Creatures without skins are not allowed to enter."

Torto went home and brooded. God came up to him.

"Well, Torto," said God kindly, "would you like a skin yet?"

Torto thought deeply.

"Yes," he said at last, "I would like a skin. But only a very special sort of skin."

"And what sort of a skin is that?" asked God.

"I would like," said Torto, "a skin that I can put on, or take off, just whenever I please."

God frowned.

"I'm afraid," he said, "I have none like that."

"Then make one," replied Torto. "You're God."

God went away and came back within an hour.

"Do you want a beautiful skin?" he asked. "Or do you mind if it's very ugly?"

"I don't care what sort of a skin it is," said Torto, "so long as I can take it off and put it back on again just whenever I please."

God went away again, and again came back within an hour.

"Here it is. That's the best I can do."

"What's this!" cried Torto. "But it's horrible!"

"Take it or leave it," said God, and walked away.

Torto examined the skin. It was tough, rough, and stiff.

"It's like a coconut," he said. "With holes in it."

And so it was. Only it was shiny. When he tried it on, he found it quite snug. It had only one disadvantage. He could move only very slowly in it.

"What's the hurry?" he said to himself then. "When it comes to moving, who can move faster than me?"

And he laughed. Suddenly he felt delighted. Away he went to where the animals were still running their races.

As he came near to them, he began to think that perhaps his skin was a little rough and ready. But he checked himself:

"Why should I dress up for them?" he said. "This rough old thing will do. The races are the important thing."

Tiger lowered his notice and stared in dismay as Torto swaggered past him. All the animals were now turning and staring, nudging each other, and turning, and staring.

"That's a change, anyway," thought Torto.

Then, as usual, he entered for all the races.

···

The animals began to talk and laugh among themselves as they pictured Torto trying to run in his heavy new clumsy skin.

"He'll look silly, and then how we'll laugh." And they all laughed.

But when he took his skin off at the starting post, their laughs turned to frowns.

He won all the races, then climbed back into his skin to collect the prizes. He strutted in front of all the animals.

"Now it's my turn to be snobbish," he said to himself.

Then he went home, took off his skin, and slept sweetly. Life was perfect for him.

This went on for many years. But though the animals would now speak to him, they remembered what he had been. That didn't worry Torto, however. He became very fond of his skin. He began to keep it on at night when he came home after the races. He began to do everything in it, except actually race. He crept around slowly, smiling at the leaves, letting the days pass.

There came a time when there were no races for several weeks. During all this time Torto

never took his skin off once. Until, when the first race came round at last, he found he could not take his skin off at all, no matter how he pushed and pulled. He was stuck inside it. He strained and squeezed and gasped, but it was no use. He was stuck.

However, he had already entered for all the races, so he had to run.

He lined up, in his skin, at the start, alongside Hare, Greyhound, Cheetah, and Ostrich. They were all great runners, but usually he could beat the lot of them easily. The crowd stood agog.

"Perhaps," Torto was thinking, "my skin won't make much difference. I've never really tried to run my very fastest in it."

151

•••

The starter's pistol cracked, and away went Greyhound, Hare, Cheetah, and Ostrich, neck and neck. Where was Torto?

The crowd roared with laughter.

Torto had fallen on his face and had not moved an inch. At his first step, cumbered by his stiff, heavy skin, he had fallen on his face. But he tried. He climbed back onto his feet and made one stride, slowly, then a second stride, and was just about to make a third when the race was over and Cheetah had won. Torto had moved not quite three paces. How the crowd laughed!

And so it was with all the races. In no one race did Torto manage to make more than three steps before it was over.

The crowd was enjoying itself. Torto was weeping with shame.

After the last race, he turned to crawl home. He only wanted to hide. But though the other animals had let him go off alone when he had the prizes, now they came alongside him, in a laughing, mocking crowd.

"Who's the slowest of all the creatures?" they shouted.

"Torto is!"

"Who's the slowest of all the creatures?"

"Torto is!" all the way home.

After that, Torto tried to keep himself out of sight, but the other animals never let him rest. Whenever any of them chanced to see him, they would shout at the tops of their voices:

"Who's the slowest of all the creatures?"

And every other creature within hearing would answer, at the tops of their voices:

"Torto is!"

And that is how Torto came to be known as "Tortoise."

"That's just how I felt when I first came to this field."

Two Wise Children

Robert Graves

A boy called Bill Brain, a minister's son, lived in New England near the sea. One Tuesday morning in summer he went for a walk through the fields, picking blueberries into a tin can. Half a mile from home he passed a big house which some newcomers to the town had just bought. They were Colonel and Mrs. Deeds and he had first met them on the Sunday before, outside his father's church. Colonel Deeds watched birds, and Mrs. Deeds drove fast cars. Avis, their only daughter, had fair pigtails, a sunburned face, white teeth, and a snub nose. Bill felt shy with girls, having no sisters. But something about Avis had struck him at once. It seemed as though he had known her for years and years, and as though they shared a big secret. And he guessed that she felt the same about him because her smile wasn't just a polite smile of welcome, but one that meant, "Oh, there you are at last!" Avis was eight, and Bill two years older!

The day before, when Bill had awakened from a bad dream, he remembered that Avis had come into it, and that he had dreamed the same thing two or three times since Christmas. He couldn't say exactly what had happened in the dream, except that he was being watched by a huge, jeering crowd while some big black animal tried to kill him, and that suddenly Avis flew down from a tree and said, "It's all right, Bill. The bandages are in father's medicine chest." He thought to himself, "What a crazy dream!" Yet it still seemed real to him in a way, and he couldn't laugh it off. He couldn't even bring himself to tell his mother and father about it at breakfast.

Well, now it was Tuesday morning. And as he passed the Deeds's big house with the blueberry can slung around his neck, he suddenly said to himself, "How could I have dreamed about Avis

long before I met her? Or did I just dream that I had already dreamed the same thing two or three times before?" Bill could see nobody in the Deeds's garden, and he didn't like to shout "Avis, are you there?" So he went on towards Robson's farm, which lay hidden behind a wood. The best blueberry bushes grew on a small rocky hill nearby and he went up it, picking fast into the can, which was already half full. A few minutes later he reached the top and saw something very curious on the other side.

There stood Avis
on the back of Robson's white horse,
with one foot lifted like a dancer's, her arms
spread out, and a hay rake balanced upright on
her chin, while the horse galloped around
the field!

"That girl must have worked in a circus," he
thought. But in case she might not like being
watched, he went back behind the hilltop, picked
blueberries for another five minutes or so, and
then came up again whistling loudly. Avis had got
down from the white horse and now sat on a
rock with her head bent over some work or other.

She heard Bill's whistle.

"There you are at last," she said.
"I expected you five minutes ago.
Where have you been?"

But Bill was looking at a small
square of white linen which
she held crumpled in her hand.
"Is that what you have been sewing?"
he asked. "Let me look!"

"Oh, it's not worth anything," Avis said.
"This is the first time I've done needlework.
I borrowed mother's colored silks. It's taken me
most of the morning."

"What else have you done?"

"Oh, eaten a few blueberries and tried riding
Farmer Robson's horse."

"I suppose that was the first time you ever rode
a horse?" Bill asked, to tease her.

But Avis said seriously, "Yes, the first time ever,
but I got along quite well."

Bill took the crumpled square of linen from
her hand, and found on it the most wonderful
needlework he had ever seen. It was a silk picture
of flowers and butterflies sewn in about thirty
different colors with hundreds of tiny stitches.

···

Only one flower and half a butterfly were not yet finished.

"Did you copy a pattern?" Bill asked.

"No," said Avis.

Bill looked her straight in the eyes. He said, "I saw you riding the horse. I hope you don't mind. And now there's this marvelous needlework. Explain, please. . . ."

"Oh, I didn't mind being watched by *you*," said Avis. "And there's nothing much to explain, really. I wanted to do a circus act, so I just did it, because I knew how. And I wanted to make this needlework picture in colored silks, so I just did it because I knew how."

"Oh, I *see!*" said Bill.

"What do you see?" asked Avis.

"I see what's happened to you. It's like what happened to me last spring in a field near our house. I was alone, and the dogwoods had just begun to flower, and hundreds of birds sang, and the world seemed changed and *right*."

"Yes," said Avis. "That's just how I felt when I first came to this field. Go on!"

Bill went on, "Suddenly I found that I knew everything. I had only to tilt my head a little and

160

ask myself any question I pleased, and the answer came at once."

"What *sort* of things?"

"Well, I had often wondered who first built our house and when he built it. So I tilted my head and knew that a Scotch blacksmith called Sawney Todd and his son Robb had built it in 1656. And somehow I knew that if I dug down four or five inches under my left heel, I'd find an old gold brooch belonging to Ruth Todd, Sawney's wife. So I cut out a piece of turf with my knife and found the brooch. It had 'R.T. 1654' scratched on the back."

"Did that scare you? *I* got a scare at first by things going marvelously right like that. I'm used to them now."

"It did scare me a little. Then I went home and there was my Uncle Tim arguing with Father about some law business. They had a lot of papers spread on the table, written in very difficult English. Uncle Tim was being rather rude to my father, so I said, 'You're wrong, I'm afraid, Uncle Tim.' And I picked the papers up, read out one of the most difficult ones to him, and showed him just where he had made his mistake. They both looked at me in such surprise that I got all red and explained, 'You see, I know everything today.' Father frowned at me for boasting, but Uncle Tim laughed and asked, 'All right, Bill, if you know everything, what horse will win the big race on Saturday?' I tilted my head, and then told him, 'A big black horse called Gladiator will win. It's ridden by Sam Smile.'"

Avis interrupted. "I don't *know* everything, Bill; it's just that I can *do* everything. It's a bit different. Do you still know everything?"

Bill sighed. "No, I don't, Avis. That's what I want to warn you about, if you don't mind.

Take care not to let anyone but me into your new secret. I made a terrible mistake over mine."

"What sort of a mistake?" Avis asked.

"It had to do with money. My Uncle Tim went off to town and bet a hundred dollars that Gladiator would win the race, and it did. He made a thousand dollars from the bet, and gave me a ten-dollar bill for myself, and told all his friends about my knowing everything. One of them asked me what horse would win the next big race. I tried to tell him, but somehow no answer came. Then I hoped that I'd know if I saw a list of all the horses that were going to run.

The man showed me a list, but still I couldn't tell him the winner, so I guessed a horse called Clever Bill—and it came in last! That was in May, and I have never since felt that I know everything. I'm sure I lost my magic by taking the ten dollars. Magic and money don't mix."

Avis said, "You mean, Bill, that I oughtn't to tell anyone, even my mother, that I can do whatever I like? Just in case her friends try to make money out of me?"

Bill nodded. "I'm sure that's how it is."

Avis looked a little sad as she said, "Thank you, Bill. I'll have to change my plans. I'd thought of winning the hundred-dollar skating competition at the New Year Ice Carnival—I haven't ever skated, but it looks fun. And I'd thought of teaching my dog to sing real songs while I played the guitar.

And I'd thought of growing a new red flower
with my name written in white on its petals,
which would come out only on June tenth—
that's my birthday."

"Mine too," said Bill.

"And flying round and round the White
House at Washington, just to amuse the
President. Like this . . ."

Avis suddenly jumped
into the air, glided around
a big maple tree,

picking a leaf from the top branch as she went by, and then lay down in the air about three feet from the ground as if she were on a sofa. She said, "I'm not showing off, Bill, I promise. I'm just telling you how easy it is for me to do things."

"*Please* be careful, Avis," said Bill. "If your magic went away, you'd feel so lost and empty inside."

"But it's far more fun to do things like this if someone is watching and knows that I really can do them. I'm lucky to have *you*, Bill. I trust you."

"Oh, I wish, I wish, I wish I hadn't taken Uncle Tim's money," said Bill. "I wish I knew everything again. It would make life so much easier, especially school."

"Maybe you'll get the magic back one day," said Avis.

"I doubt it," said Bill. "Anyhow don't lose yours! Don't let your father and mother find out that you aren't just an ordinary little girl. Don't fly up to your bedroom through the window when they may be looking. Use the stairs! And I'd better keep this bit of needlework hidden. Your mother might ask questions about it."

⋯

Avis gave Bill a hug and said, "I *do* like you, Bill. You're my favorite friend of all. Thank you, thank you!"

Bill said, "By the way, Avis, did you dream of me before we met?"

"Oh, yes, ever since I can remember. I guess that's because we have the same birthday."

She ran off, and Bill thought, "I'm glad she didn't fly home. Farmer Robson's in the next field and might have seen her."

Avis kept Bill's advice all that summer. They saw a lot of each other. Since she didn't really care about making money, or showing off to strangers, she might never have lost her magic but for another stupid mistake of Bill's.

It happened like this. One day he thought, "Maybe I could learn Avis's sort of *doing* magic, although I've lost my own *knowing* magic." He walked towards Robson's farm, and there he saw Robson's bull: a big, mean, black brute which was kept in a special field with stone walls and a padlocked iron gate. Bill had read about bullfights. He knew that in Spain the bullfighter goes into a ring where thousands of people sit watching all around. When the bull rushes up, the bullfighter holds out a red cape and steps aside to let the bull charge it instead of him. Then he keeps on making the bull charge his cape, time after time, all around the ring, and everyone cheers. And then . . .

"I'll try it,"
Bill said.
He climbed
the gate, walked
towards the bull,
and took off his brown
jacket to act as a cape—but
forgot that he was wearing a red shirt
underneath! Bulls hate that color, and instead of
charging the jacket which Bill held out, Robson's
bull went straight for the shirt, knocked him
down, stuck a horn into his leg, and tossed him
high in the air.

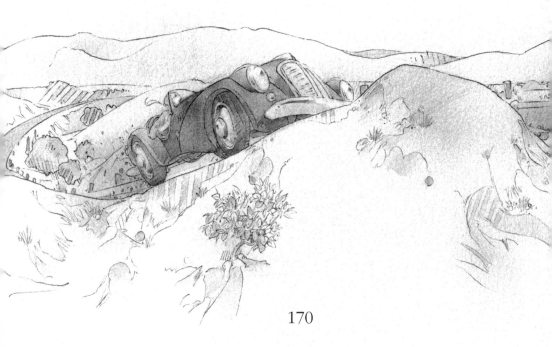

•••

That would have been the end of Bill, if his dream hadn't come true. Avis suddenly appeared when he had been horned three times. Somehow she tamed the bull, laid Bill (who had fainted) across the bull's shoulders, jumped up behind, and made the bull gallop back to her home!

When they got there, she called to Colonel Deeds for help. But he was bird-watching somewhere, and Mrs. Deeds had gone shopping in the station wagon. So Avis grabbed bandages and all sorts of first-aid stuff from the family medicine chest. Then she bandaged Bill's wounds, stopped the bleeding, and put Bill into the back of her mother's sports car.

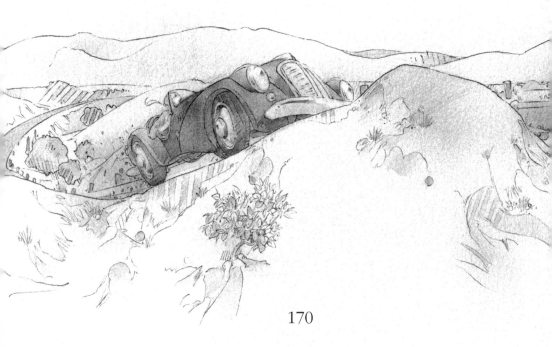

In spite of the state police who tried to stop her at the crossroads, she drove ten miles at full speed to the nearest hospital, where the doctors took charge of Bill. She had forgotten about the bull, which ate most of the roses in the garden and made holes in the lawn with its hooves.

Avis had no chance of keeping the news quiet. The police wanted to know how she had managed to drive her mother's car so fast and well, and the doctors wanted to know who had bandaged Bill's leg in such a clever way, and Farmer Robson wanted to know how his bull had gotten over a locked gate! Reporters came from all the

newspapers and asked her more questions and more questions, and she kept on saying "I don't know . . . I don't know," because she had promised Bill to be careful, and it was true that she didn't know *how* she had done it all without learning. They took photographs of her and put her name in the papers as EIGHT-YEAR-OLD GIRL WONDER.

Soon the Governor called at the Deeds's house and asked to see Avis. Mrs. Deeds was very proud of the visit and let the Governor pester Avis with more questions until she got tired of answering "I don't know, I don't know." At last she burst into tears and said, "Oh, *please* go away, or you'll spoil everything! Can't you leave me and my magic alone?"

"Oh, so you do it by magic?" said the Governor, giving her a huge box of candy. "How very interesting! You mustn't cry! Will you come and show us some magic at my little girl's birthday party next Saturday?"

And before Avis could say "No, I won't! It's a secret," Mrs. Deeds answered for her. "Of course, Mr. Governor, my daughter will be *delighted*." This was how Avis lost her magic.

When Bill got out of the hospital, none the worse, she blamed him for having spoiled her fun. But she *had* saved his life, which was the important thing; and he would always be her favorite friend.

Besides, in some ways it was a relief to be ordinary again, like Bill.

ACKNOWLEDGMENTS

All possible care has been taken to trace ownership and secure permission for each selection in this series. The Great Books Foundation wishes to thank the following authors, publishers, and representatives for permission to reprint copyrighted material:

The Dream Weaver, from EL JARDÍN DE LAS SIETE PUERTAS, by Concha Castroviejo. Copyright © 1961 by Concha Castroviejo. Reprinted by permission of María Antonia Seijo Castroviejo. English translation by Helen Lane. Translation copyright © 2002 by the Great Books Foundation.

Jean Labadie's Big Black Dog, from THE TALKING CAT AND OTHER STORIES OF FRENCH CANADA, by Natalie Savage Carlson. Copyright © 1952 by Natalie Savage Carlson. Reprinted by permission of HarperCollins Publishers.

THE UPSIDE-DOWN BOY, by Juan Felipe Herrera. Copyright © 2000 by Juan Felipe Herrera. Reprinted by permission of Children's Book Press.

THE GREEN MAN, by Gail E. Haley. Copyright © 1979 by Gail E. Haley. Reprinted by permission of the author.

The Ugly Duckling, from IT'S PERFECTLY TRUE AND OTHER STORIES, by Hans Christian Andersen. Translation copyright © 1937 by Paul Leyssac; renewed 1965 by Mary Rehan. Reprinted by permission of Harcourt, Inc.

WHITE WAVE, by Diane Wolkstein. Copyright © 1979 by Diane Wolkstein. Reprinted by permission of the author.

THE MOUSEWIFE, by Rumer Godden. Copyright © 1951, 1979 by Rumer Godden. First appeared in THE MOUSEWIFE, published by Viking Penguin, Inc. Reprinted by permission of Curtis Brown, Ltd.

How the Tortoise Became, from HOW THE WHALE BECAME AND OTHER STORIES, by Ted Hughes. Copyright © 1963 by Ted Hughes. Reprinted by permission of Faber and Faber, Ltd., and Orchard Books, a division of Scholastic, Inc.

TWO WISE CHILDREN, by Robert Graves. Copyright © 1966 by Harlan Quist, Inc. Reprinted by permission of the Estate of Robert Graves and Carcanet Press.